# Victorian Furniture

## Styles and Prices

Robert and Harriett Swedberg

Books by Robert W. and Harriett Swedberg
*Off Your Rocker*
*Victorian Furniture Styles and Prices*
*Country Pine Furniture Styles and Prices*

ISBN 0-87069-327-1

Library of Congress Catalog No. 80-51584

Photographs: by the authors
Printing and Enlarging: Tom Luse

Published by

Wallace-Homestead Book Company
1912 Grand Avenue
Des Moines, Iowa 50309

# Dedication

The authors, Harriett and Robert, dedicate this book to the countless friends and acquaintances who have in many ways contributed facts and fancies which have enabled us over the years to gain the knowledge to successfully impart to others our love and appreciation of the world of antiques.

# Acknowledgments

The authors sincerely thank the following individuals and dealers who generously assisted us as we compiled this book. We also appreciate the help of those dealers and individuals who did not wish to have their names included.

Bright View Antiques & Collectibles (Evelyn Maxwell), Milan, Illinois

Nancy and Bob Coopman

Dr. and Mrs. Todd Frisch

Historic House Ltd., Antique & Art Gallery (Dale and Teresa Hoffman), Moline, Illinois

Joseph Huntoon Homestead, registered as a National Historic Site, Moline, Illinois

Jim and Lu Ann Lavine

Libra Antiques (Barbara Emery), Moline, Illinois

Ray and Jane (Lundeen) Miller

Ron and Dorothy Mlekush

Sheila and Howard Moore

Ethel Myers

Virginia and Harold Peterson

Mary Rachael Antiques (Mary Levery), Washington, Illinois

Mr. and Mrs. Carl Ropp

Dian and Joe Schuh

Marion Slocum's Antiques, Andalusia, Illinois

Robert and Wilma Smith

Cheryl Swedberg

Mr. and Mrs. Richard Taber and Christian

Village Square Antiques (Glen M., Jerry, and Theresa Nance), Pocahontas, Illinois

Terry and Karen Watson, Cody and Adam

# Preface

"Your book should be called *Walnut Victorian Furniture,* not *Victorian Furniture, Styles and Prices,*" a friend remarked. "It ignores the other woods which were utilized."

While there are a few pieces that are not walnut in Book I, this criticism is correct. The contents adhere mainly to one wood. Metal, too, was omitted. Lacy iron garden benches and ornamental beds of brass or iron were over-looked and country furniture was forgotten. So . . . Book II will attempt to include types which were neglected previously. Catalogues of 1873 and 1876 were examined diligently. (The first photographs shown for sales promotion at Grand Rapids, Michigan, date to 1862, not too many years after the daguerreotype process was announced in 1839 and improvements followed.) Instead of taking room-to-room views, styles receive stress. This adds a new dimension.

A long distance telephone call from Alabama came from a couple who is restoring an anti-bellum home to its pre-1861 graciousness. They eagerly bid on a parlor suite, its frames identical to one depicted in Book I. Elated when the price did not exceed that listed in our book, they showed the auctioneer that the amount he received was low in comparison, and called to share their news with strangers. They desired to know what fabrics and colors would appear authentic, and there again information was requested which readers seek. This book provides answers. Were you aware that haircloth, frequently utilized by upholsterers, is available today? We are accustomed to black, but it was and is possible to secure this stiff fabric made from horsehair in colors and small patterns.

A dealer in the deep South extended an invitation to come photograph some of her prized possessions. She wanted her shop represented in the book. Her pictures would have been a welcome addition but she was on a buying expedition at the time it would have been possible to schedule a visit to her.

Other requests have been for prices on furniture "in the rough" (pieces bought as is which require attention before they can be placed in homes).

Another collector wanted a section on "convertibles," pieces which have been changed, such as tables cut down to form coffee tables, or altered beds.

And, from Washington, D.C., Kiplinger's "Changing Times" magazine listed Book I as one of the price guides to consult when investigating the cost of passé furniture.

We hope we've made Book II a practical source book.

# Main Characteristics of Nineteenth Century Furniture

**Empire 1815 - 1840.** Age of mahogany. Rosewood and ebony utilized also. Marble tops. Heavy lines. Thick lyre bases and scrolls. Symmetrical. Rectangular shapes. Ogee frames. Cornices on secretaries and cupboards. Beading. Wings as feet on sofas. Acanthus leaf and laurel branch swags. Cornucopias. Round wooden pulls or lion head back plates with ring pulls. Mainly handmade. Inspired by French Emperor Napoleon (ruled 1799 - 1815 intermittently).

**Spool 1820 - 1870.** Machine made. Turnings which resembled a series of spools, buttons, or knobs in a row. Hardwoods and square lines early; rounded bed ends and pine after 1850. (Still made today.)

**Hitchcock Fancy Chairs 1820 - 1850.** Mass produced. Hitchcock helped start the modern factory system. Generic term for fancy chairs customarily painted. Cornucopia and flowers. Powdered gold accents. Mixed woods. (Still made today.)

**Gothic 1820 - 1850s,** again in 1870s. Not much made. Church look. Pointed spires resembling old fashioned church steeple. Light look. Arches. Tracery resembled church window.

**Louis XV 1840 - 1865.** Imitated original Louis XV style (French king, 1715-1774). Rococo carvings (rock, shell, flora, fauna). Curves. Straight lines avoided. Elliptical shapes more than round. Marble tops. Fancy fruit, nut, and leaf carved handles. Upholstery with spiral springs. Cabriole legs. Finger roll frames. Walnut, some rosewood and mahogany.

**Renaissance 1850 - 1885.** Tall. High bedsteads, secretary desks, china cabinets. Machine made, frequently with hand carved details. Elaborate. Extravagant. Carved crests and pediments. Roundels. Huge dressing case mirrors. Carved wooden pulls continued. Ebony and gilt handles (tear drops). Pedestals with cluttered bases. Turned finials. Urns. Columbia (carved head of a woman symbolizing the U.S.), circa 1876. Mainly walnut, which grew scarce by 1880s. Marble tops.

**Cottage Furniture 1845 - 1890.** Painted or artificially grained. Country type. Inexpensive. Pastoral scenes, flowers, birds. Pine. Sometimes had walnut handles and carved applied decorations.

**Eastlake 1870 - 1890.** Eastlake revolted against elaborate, machine made, sometimes poorly constructed furniture. Rectangular lines. Straight. Incised lines and chip carving. U.S. took English Eastlake and added appendages until his simple look became cluttered. Walnut.

**Metal 1850 - 1900.** Iron bed frames. Brass or iron with brass trim or plating was popular at the end of the 1800s. Brass beds are made today.

**Wicker 1850 - 1920.** Generic term for fibers such as rattan, reed, willow, and paper twisted spirals.

**Exit walnut.**

**Golden Oak 1890 - 1920.** Yellowish color. Pressed brass bail handles. Pressed design on chair backs. Round pedestal extension dining room tables. China cabinets with convex glass. Claw feet. Rectangular dining tables with bulbous legs. Combination furniture such as beds which fold into chests or desks, drop lid desks with bookcase sides. Being made today.

**Mission Oak 1895 - 1910.** Utilitarian. Stained dark. Heavy, straight, strong, square lines.

**Birdseye Maple 1895 - early 1900s.** Veneer which resembles the eye of a bird. Found more in maple than other woods. Frequently has a Louis XV style.

**Maple turn of century.** Stained red with aniline dye to resemble mahogany. Heavy, sturdy lines.

**Shakers.** Religious society which made furniture with beautiful simple lines from the late 1700s through the 1800s. Sold mainly rockers with woven seats. Slat backs or woven backs.

**Patented furniture.** Many varieties. High chair which converted to stroller, bed which folded into a desk, platform rockers.

**Victorians** had new machines and enjoyed borrowing from all sources as they made furniture. An Oriental feel came after 1875 with bamboo furniture or lacquer work or inlays. Dragons could be decorations.

**Windsor chairs** were introduced into America about 1725 and have remained around ever since. Multi-spindled backs. Splayed legs, plank seats. Mixed woods.

Remember, periods overlap or there are transitional pieces which combine the look of two periods. Note also that some furniture endures without many distinguishing features. For example, millions of cane bottom side chairs with slat backs were manufactured, and washstands kept the same look consistently. This means that it is difficult to place a definite year tag on furniture and the term "circa" (around) is a good one to utilize.

# Contents

# Chapter 1
# Let Your Price Book Be Your Guide

To guide means to lead the way, direct, or conduct. This book seeks to guide readers, helping them identify various types of Victorian furniture and suggesting current prices.

Prices, prices, prices. What determines the cost of an object? First of all — there must be a buyer who wants what is being sold and is willing to pay the amount asked. Supply and demand are important. Scarce yet desirable articles will command more money.

*How are prices arrived at for this book?* Research. Travel. Inquiry. For Book I questionnaires were sent out and crisscrossed the country from Alaska to Florida and Maine to Hawaii, and the results were compiled to present a picture of popular prices. This 1976 survey helps as a bottom step reference on an ascending stairway as costs spiral upward. Prices jotted down at popular auctions, estate sales, shops, flea markets, malls, or shows give guidance. Talks with collectors and discussion with dealers add insight. A visit to Grand Rapids, Michigan, furniture capital of the United States in the last century helped and provided old catalogues for research assistance.

Pricing is complex. Recently a concerned woman telephoned because a friend was moving and was getting rid of various possessions. What is a wicker baby buggy worth? She felt her friend was listing hers too low since it was not tagged so high as one at an antique show. Consider these facts. A dealer may keep objects for years without selling them and he or she has daily bills to pay. A shopper who attends a yard or garage sale hopes to find a bargain, and unless the object is irresistible, shuns that which is expensive. The carriage owner has to sell out in a few days. If she expects total value on all her merchandise, she may not achieve her purpose. Who needs or wants an archaic baby buggy? A doll collector? A new mother or grandparent? Someone decorating a turn-of-the-century home? The market is limited, and the owner has to wait for the proper purchaser to appear.

Condition is a factor since articles which go to shows are generally physically fit, ready to be placed in a home setting without further attention. Is the friend's buggy in peak shape?

Age needs to be considered. A dealer from the far West did not desire to haul home round, woven under-and-over factory-produced wicker. "That won't sell," he declared. In his locale, potential customers picked more elderly versions.

Is the carriage baby or doll size? Is it a stroller, a pull cart, an English pram? Close your eyes. What do you see when someone says wicker baby buggy? Everyone's retinas snap different pictures so a telephone appraisal is inaccurate.

Now hear this. There are dealers in the middle portion of the country who state that they no longer stock walnut because it doesn't move. One says, "Young people seek oak. Vans from the West Coast and the South load up with oak so we don't bother with walnut any more." Or, others state, "We like walnut but have to have oak in order to meet expenses."

But, there are still those who prefer the dark rich dignified glow of walnut, cherry, mahogany, and rosewood, pieces that are a hundred and carry their age well.

Carefully crafted, unusual articles sell. The highly carved features of Renaissance attract, and a close neck-to-neck in appeal are the curvaceous Louis XV substyles. Meanwhile, some dealers find the boxy lines of designer Charles L. Eastlake, embellished by the steam-run machines that were new when Victorian furniture was young, are attracting greater value than previously.

Think about condition for a moment! What is a settee frame worth which is ready to be reupholstered? A similar sofa frame has worn fabric and needs recovering, but all of the underneath work is satisfactory. How is that priced? The latter piece has greater value as it is usable and has the springs and supports to which to attach the upholstery. The following pictures illustrate the differences.

*Finger roll back, 5' 9" outside measurement. (Walnut)*
**$650.00 - 700.00**

*Finger roll back, 5' 3" outside measurement. (Walnut)*
**$200.00 - 250.00**

Differences can also be seen if you compare the prices of the following side chair, gentleman's chair, and lady's chair with their completed versions in Chapter 3.

*Side chair, fruit and leaf carved crest, serpentine apron. (Walnut)*
**$65.00 - 80.00**

*Gentleman's chair, oval back, finger roll, open arms. (Walnut)*
**$175.00 - 200.00**

*Lady's chair, oval back, finger roll. (Walnut)*
**$175.00 - 200.00**

*Butternut chest, brass escutcheons, porcelain pulls, bread-*
*board top. 28½" wide, 13½" deep, 32" high.*
**$225.00 - 250.00.**

*Hall tree, 6' 11", missing pediment, applied ornaments,*
*veneer panels, marble top over drawer, (Walnut)*
**$350.00 - 500.00 as is;**
**$750.00 - 1,000.00 refinished.**

## Prices Affected by Alterations

Some articles of furniture may be missing essential parts. For example, a chair may be without one of its demi-arms, a washstand may have lost its original splash back of wood or marble, a dresser may be without its handkerchief boxes. None of these crippled pieces, of course, can demand top value. The walnut halltree as pictured with the absent pediment would have an arbitrary one hundred dollars subtracted from its value. Quite often a missing crest indicates that the article of furniture would not fit into a certain location. The top was consequently removed, stored, and in many cases never again found.

A petite, four-drawer butternut chest with porcelain pulls had its top sawed off at each end so that it could fit into a required space. It was repaired by adding breadboard ends. What does this mean dollarwise? Because such an insignificant percentage of the piece was changed, the price difference would be negligible, for structurally you have the chest in its entirety. Had the drawer front been replaced or the entire top been added anew, then the price would significantly decrease.

13

A work table is minus its base shelf and has a handle replaced. How would this be priced in comparison with another complete unit? Handles are often switched and seldom does this change affect the price as long as the replaced handles fit the style and period of the piece. The shelf would mean that a part of the original structure was gone, and consequently an arbitrary ten to fifteen per cent of its value, if otherwise perfect, should be subtracted.

## The Changelings

Is there any price loss when an attractive cane chair is given an upholstered seat and back? A reader requested information about furniture which has been altered. Such a change would affect the originality of the chair, and as a result the value would decrease, for the person no longer has a cane seat and cane back chair. Considering the current cost of caning, the approximate price to put this chair back in its original condition would be in excess of fifty dollars.

*Rocking chair, shield back, hip rest, shell motif on back crest, 15½" to seat, 34" high. (Walnut)*
**$155.00 - 175.00.**

*Bedside stand, 22½" wide, 16" deep, 29" high. (Walnut)*
**$85.00 - 110.00.**

Does a marble table retain its full value when it is cut down to coffee table height? Because coffee tables are a contemporary innovation and do not represent a Victorian creation, the value is less than the original table, but not substantially so because there has been and is a continuing demand for such tables in front of sofas. However, with the Victorian-advocate generation waning, today's coffee table is more apt to be a pine chest or carpenter's trunk than a cut down walnut parlor table.

14

*Cut down oval top, 29″ x 19½″, 17½″ high. (Walnut)*
**$135.00 - 150.00**

*Below: Youth bed, replaced frame, floral carving on headboard. (Maple)*
**$180.00 - 210.00**

How do you deal with three-quarters beds that have been converted to singles? That is to say — is some of the value lost? Obviously, such a re-creation has less value, but in the world of antiques individual tastes and desires dictate what you can or cannot do with a particular piece of furniture. If a single bed is what you want, let it be done, for it is you who will live with it. A Midwestern school teacher had a mid-nineteenth century maple rope bed but had no use for it as is, so she asked the male author of this pair to fashion a head board from it for a frame she owned. When the job was completed to her satisfaction, she not only received continuing compliments on her changed bed, but two small table lamps and a floor lamp were made from the left over parts. A purist would most certainly frown upon this.

15

Is it proper to extend beds so that they can accommodate seventy-five inch mattresses? Some people substitute long metal rails. Others dowel or screw a carefully crafted addition to a rail so today's tall people can use the bed in comfort. Is this wrong to do?

Common sense indicates that a six footer has to scrunch to sleep in an old time bedstead. If the frame is to be of use and not merely to be looked at, it must be extended in a manner which preserves the bed best and still keeps it functional. This should not destroy value.

### Marriages

Here's a piece that's a marriage — two unrelated items united as one. The base is a dry sink. The top is a turn-of-the-century Hoosier-type cupboard. If a dealer were to sell this to a novice as an authentic article, there would be a problem. When a house owner enjoys her unrelated objects attractively displayed, she will not object. Marriages for resale are not recommended.

*Pine dry sink with Hoosier cabinet top. Sink 50½" wide, 20" deep, 35½" high. Hoosier top 47" wide, 9½" deep, 30" high.*
**$475.00 - 525.00.**

16

## Repair Work

A cane chair has a broken seat. Should it be repaired? If someone wants to sit on it — yes. If not, it remains a decorative space taker incapable of fulfilling its useful function.

*Rocking chair, rectangular caned back, demi-arms, U-shaped caned seat, 16″ to seat, 35″ high. (Maple stained walnut)*
**$150.00 - 175.00.**

It is not wise to purchase objects which are too battered and beat up. The necessary restoration, especially if replacing parts is required, may be too costly or destroy value. If it's a period piece, perhaps it is worth salvaging. If not, you may end up with a costly nothing much.

## What about Refinishing?

You, the user, may be the loser moneywise if you refinish antique pieces. Often, as the color flows down the drain, so does the dollar. There are purists who demand and pay top price for pristine items, and there are authorities who ask, "Why does an antique have to look new?" Why shouldn't it carry the wrinkles of age which show it has a history behind it and retain the stains, varnish, shellac, paint, or other protective coating originally put upon it?

One Iowa dealer prides herself on selling her wooden objects as is. She remarks, "Customers say I have the only shop in the Midwest with furniture intact that has its original coating which adds authenticity. I don't strip anything."

There are some who disagree. A collector expressed her ideas in this manner: "I figure the first owner didn't use a dirty dough tray but had it look nice in her home. I want mine to be cleaned up so it will appear as attractive as possible."

17

How much would you pay for the cupboard shown in its present state? What would the refinished price be? The decision to refinish or not depends on the owner's preference.

*Kitchen cupboard, set back top, applied panels on doors and drawers, molded cornice, 37" wide, 22½" deep, 6' 5½" high. (Walnut)*

**$350.00 - 400.00 as is;**
**$600.00 - 700.00 refinished.**

On period pieces, circa pre-1830, be aware that refinishing a piece with original finish intact can decrease value, but, cleaning is permissible. A book such as *Off Your Rocker* by the Swedbergs, published by Wallace-Homestead, gives specific details on the care of antiques. Here is a brief account on cleaning passé items.

When a piece has a build-up of wax, a turpentine or paint thinner washing using clean soft cloths immersed in this liquid and wrung well removes it. Dry, as you work, with rags. (See bathing instructions for procedure.) This is done first when required.

Oil Bath
(boiled linseed, mineral, or pure lemon oil, etc.):
Using extra fine (triple 000) steel wool, rub a small section diligently. Remove loosened dirt with a clean, dry cotton cloth with no buttons or abrasive decorations. Continue until entire surface is cleansed. Many rags are required.

Water Bath:
After removing wax, if required, place a little detergent (handful) in a gallon of barely warm water. Add 3 capfuls of turpentine or paint thinner and 2 tablespoons of oil (see kinds listed above). Scrub a small section with a rag dampened in the mixture, wringing the rag well so as not to saturate the wood. Rinse with clean water and dry thoroughly with clean cloths as you work. Proceed until the entire piece has been gone over. This removes the grime, but veneer or inlay might require special care because water loosens glue.

Sometimes painted pieces such as country furniture, factory made in the last half of the nineteenth century, wear a discolored coat of sticky shellac to which dirt clings. It can be cleaned by rubbing small areas with triple 000 steel wool (very fine) and alcohol. Rub well. Remove the loosened material immediately with a clean dry cloth with no buttons or abrasive ornaments on it. Have an abundant supply of rags and discard them as they become dirty and tacky. Continue working on small sections until all have been cleaned. Protect the painted surface by applying a paste wax according to manufacturer's directions.

On all these methods, if you feel insecure, *test them on a small inconspicuous area* and stop if you do not approve of the results. A protective paste wax coating may be applied. Never use furniture polish which contains silicon. It can leave dark spots in the wood.

# Chapter 2
## Ponderous Empire (Circa 1815-1840)

It is necessary to make an entrance into the Victorian era through the Empire which preceded it. Furniture styles are not like the cheese which stands alone in the childhood "Farmer in the Dell" singing game. Influenced by the past, copies appear again and again, and there is no precise cut-off from one period to the next. For example, a remote cabinetmaker might make Empire-style furniture many years after Victorian curves or spool turnings won approval elsewhere. There was no instant stylizing made available by radio and television communication or rapid transportation to keep him and his customers conscious of current trends.

Transitional pieces which combine the look of the old plus the new frequently span the space between the styles; thus, the Victorian era evolves from the Empire.

Both periods were influenced by and named for European heads of state but represent vivid contrasts just as the rulers did. Bred for ruling, peaceful womanly Queen Victoria (born in 1819) headed England for sixty-three years (1837-1901) while the bellicose Emperor Napoleon, of royal Italian lineage but not the heir apparent to the French throne, predated her and was in and out of control of England's rival France for only sixteen years (1799-1815). In spite of this, his pugnacious nature earthquaked around the world.

Napoleon Bonaparte, short in stature but tall in ability as an administrator and as one of the world's greatest military commanders, was affectionately dubbed the "Little Corporal" by his devoted soldiers who followed him faithfully. Even so far away as the United States, President Thomas Jefferson dreaded the tremors of his earth-shaking, country-taking policies and was glad when this nation completed the Louisiana Purchase which ceded all France's interests on North American soil to the infant U.S. Republic and kept the emperor's land-grabbing interests focused across the Atlantic Ocean.

Dynamic, perhaps over confident to almost a vain degree, Napoleon did not wait for the Pope to place the crown on his head at the December 2, 1804, coronation ceremonies, but, seizing it from the Pontiff's hands, he first crowned himself and then his beautiful wife, Empress Josephine, thereby symbolizing his own rise to this head-of-state position. Power — that word represents ruler Napoleon Bonaparte, and it carried over into his total life pattern.

He demanded furniture made for him which depicted his image, and so his designers borrowed from ancient Egypt, Greece, and Rome to create Emperor Napoleon furniture named in his honor "Empire." The word "power" spells out a description of this masculine, massive furniture.

P - powerful, popular, often ponderous
O - ostentatious, ornate, ormolu, overly ornamented
W - weighty, world-wide influence, woods (mahogany, rosewood, ebony)
E - empire, elaborate, eclectic, Egyptian, Greek, and Roman styling
R - rectangular, rich look, rich woods

*Hall table with petticoat mirror, scroll legs, applied decoration on serpentine apron, 33" wide, 17" deep, 33½" high. (Mahogany and crotch mahogany veneer)*
**$750.00 - 850.00**

*Mirror above with painting in shield top, 28" wide, 57" high.*
**$475.00 - 525.00.**

To please the emperor's vanity, the designers selected specific emblems to exemplify Empire. What could be more significant or pride puffing than the letter "N" for Napoleon? A carved crown or bee designs on fabrics flattered Bonaparte also. A hand carved replica of the ruler's head could grace chairs, case pieces, settees, or rockers. How would you like to sleep in a bed guarded by the likeness of the "Little Corporal"? Elaborate trims frequently in the form of gilt or brass (ormolu) mounts featured wreaths, wings, swags (including acanthus leaves retained from the previous period and laurel branches), cornucopias, swords, shields, or torches. During this period of classical review in France, figures from mythology peered about or an Egyptian sphinx might stoically stare. Fabrics frequently adhered to similar designs and white silk upholstery was popular. Generally, substantial rather than soft materials prevailed, the colors deep and strong with preference shown to the primary shades of red, blue, or yellow, but deep green and brown were present too.

Woods were rich. This was the age of imported mahogany with rosewood and ebony in evidence, and the tops of some furniture were made of thick stone including marble. Stiff formal chairs and sofas did not consider sitter comfort, but the chaise lounge offered relaxation. Fall-front and table-style desks were current as were round tables with tripod or pedestal bases. The heavy rectangular shapes stressed symmetry. A column of acanthus leaf swags must be balanced so precisely as an aerial acrobatic team with a corresponding one in a like position on the opposite side. Also pairs of applied ormolu ornamentations appeared, especially in French works where decoration depended more on applied mounts than on carving. Posts, table legs, and chair arms often boasted lions, griffins (a mythical beast — half lion, half eagle), caryatids (female figures forming supporting columns), or the symbolic crown, "N", and head emblems.

*Empire chest, applied columns with acanthus leaves carved on pilaster, projection front, 45" wide, 19½" deep, 43" high. (Cherry top, walnut, crotch mahogany veneer)*

**$350.00 - 425.00.**

The United States designers had their own ideas and changed the French look to a ponderous extent with their versions appearing as a rough translation of the original. Sleigh beds with rolled back head and foot boards of equal size were a New World adaptation, deriving their name from their slight resemblance to the front of a horse pulled, snow gliding sleigh front.

Naturally, with the always prevalent name-dropping and jump-on-the-bandwagon tendency, those who sought to be a part of the "in" crowd copied this new trend until even the New York creator of delicate, dainty yet sturdy quality furniture, Duncan Phyfe (worked in the early 1790s to 1847) produced heavy Empire after 1820. Many critics felt this brought a decline in his craftmanship and did not represent his best quality offerings, but he created by hand what the public wanted and ordered. His earlier wood choice was mahogany. After 1830 he showed a preference for rosewood.

Empire furniture remained current so long as Napoleon intermittently reigned and then declined. When he lost power and was exiled from France in 1815, the Empire style went into exile too. It took time for this trend to be transported across the sea so its influence in the United States was felt from approximately 1815 to 1840. Again, always remember there is no precise cut off date since periods overlap or designers borrow freely as they experiment with new forms to create transitional pieces that incorporate both a backward and a forward look. Thus an Empire transitional sofa could have the stiff, straight, rectangular lines on the base and feet with contrasting carved and curved Victorian rolls and fruits or flowers on the top crest. The wooden frames were exposed, not fabric covered as in the modern soft sofas.

*Empire, Transitional fruit cresting, serpentine rail, applied decorations, button tied back, 6'*
*3" outside measurement. (Walnut and mahogany veneer)*
**$900.00 - 1,100.00.**

As an introduction into the Victorian era into which it interlocks, here are some examples of the Empire look.

*Empire, carved cresting, applied decorations, incised lines, tufted back and sides, 5' 1" outside measurement. (Walnut)*

**$750.00 - 900.00.**

*Empire, medallion back, carved crest, burled panels, tufted back and arms, transitional style, 5' 6" outside measurement. (Walnut)*

**$850.00 - 950.00.**

*Empire transitional, finger roll, serpentine back rail, grape carved crest, flat front legs and apron which is Empire, 5' 2½" outside measurement.*
**$400.00 - 500.00.**

*Empire game table, lyre base, scroll feet, scalloped veneered apron, 34" wide, 17" deep, 28" high. (Cherry top, mahogany veneer.)*
**$275.00 - 325.00.**

*Oak Ansonia Queen Elizabeth wall clock*
**$300.00 - 350.00.**

*Side chair, finger roll, original horsehair, tufted back. (Walnut)*
**$250.00 - 300.00.**

*Empire twelve-sided parlor table, scroll legs, beaded apron, 35¼" diameter, 28" high. (Mahogany veneer)*
**$475.00 - 525.00.**

*Game table, ogee shaped front apron, beading, squared legs, 33½" wide, 17" deep, 29" high. (Mahogany and cherry top)*
**$325.00 - 350.00.**

*Dresser, projection front, ogee shaped small handkerchief drawers and top drawer, 41" wide, 20" deep, 47" high. (Cherry)*
**$450.00 - 475.00.**

26

## Chapter 3

# Long Live Spool, Hitchcock, and Gothic Furniture!
# (Circa 1820-1849)

As has already been stated, there is no precise way to fence Victorian furniture within definite time spans and precise styles. Such divisions are arbitrary. Victoria carried the impressive title Queen of the United Kingdom of Great Britain and Ireland from 1837 to 1901 and during that time styles came and went, but various types clung to popular favor as tightly as a tick sticks to a dog's ear. Three of these persistent kinds were introduced before the young girl heir apparent ascended the throne. In this book they are classified as early Victorian, circa 1837-1849, because they indeed were found at the start of the era. These three style queens are spool furniture, Hitchcock fancy chairs, and Gothic. Spool decorations and fancy chairs are still produced.

### Early Victorian 1837-1840s

(All these were being produced before the era commenced)

### Spool Furniture (Circa 1820-1870)

Spool furniture resembles a series of spools stacked one on top of the other. Or, maybe, they are knobs or plump round buttons strung together. The result is termed "spool furniture."

The majority of the furniture produced in America during the Empire period (circa 1815-1840) was handcrafted, but spool furniture was machine made. Legs on various pieces were turned in this manner and stacks of spools sliced in half formed applied decorations on flat surfaces.

*Game table, spool legs, incised lines on apron, 36″ wide, 17½″ deep, 28½″ high. (Walnut)*
**$325.00 - 350.00.**

27

Many beds had spool turned frames, and this kind tenaciously persisted from about 1820 to 1870. Because it is more difficult to create lines of spools on a lathe to form "rounded corners," straight ends were utilized at first. Generally speaking, the early bedsteads were made from hardwoods, frequently maple, with some cherry and walnut. Pine stained dark took over after 1850.

*Tester bed, spool turnings, overall size 52"*
*wide, 76" long, 6' 6" high. (Walnut)*
**$2,100.00 - 2,350.00.**

Today dolls, toys, games, and clothes sales are promoted by associating them with television personalities and cinema stars. This is not a new trend because in the past the names of famous people have been connected with products. This proved true of spool beds which were in fashion at about the time when a famous foreign singer presented concerts in various cities throughout the United States. Ballyhooed as the Swedish Nightingale by the noted showman Phineas T. Barnum, Jenny Lind sang in "sold out" halls. She won admiration by charitable acts such as donating money to secure freedom for a former slave mother's children so the family could be reunited safely. For some reason (probably as a promotional device advocated by furniture makers or maybe because spool bedsteads were popular at the time of her 1850 tour) spool beds were associated with the singer and are referred to as "Jenny Lind" beds.

Many other articles of furniture incorporated the spool look.

Oval work table, called teaploy, one drawer, stretcher at base, 27½" x 18", 27½" high. (Walnut)

$110.00 - 135.00.

Etagère or whatnot, beading, pierced carving on back rails, serpentine drawers and doors, 42½" wide, 15½" deep, 64½" high. (Walnut and walnut veneer)
$950.00 - 1,050.00.

Day bed, spindle back and arms, pull out base to extend sleeping area, 74" wide, 24" deep, 31" high. (Maple)
$425.00 - 475.00.

29

*Baby bed, link "sausage" spindles, 36½" long, 22" wide, 30" high. (Walnut)*
**$235.00 - 275.00.**

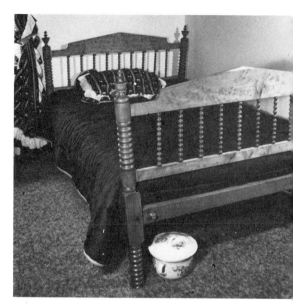

*Pin constructed bed with slats that run lengthwise, overall size 50" wide, 76" long. (Maple and curly maple)*
**$325.00 - 375.00.**

### Hitchcock Fancy Chairs (Circa 1820-1850)

While movie viewers might associate the name "Hitchcock" with surprise endings and suspense filled murder mysteries, those who enjoy antiques conjure up a picture of small painted fancy chairs. Many factories produced them, but Hitchcock's name has been retained, and the company is turning out chairs of this type currently.

Why is one man selected? Lambert Hitchcock, who began his operations around 1820, is credited with being the first to mass produce furniture in the United States. He also realized that chair legs sticking out this way and that are bulky to pack so he decided to ship chairs to retail stores unassembled. Peddlers who loaded horse-drawn wagons to carry merchandise to rural areas put the chairs together as sales were completed. Shipping charges and space were both conserved in this way.

In a day when horse-drawn vehicles sometimes got stuck in the ruts on mud-filled roads or when passengers had to get out to help push coaches up long hills, Hitchcock traveled extensively. He included visits to frontier areas as well as to cities and secured orders for his mass-made product; thus, he had a national market.

Hitchcock chairs are offsprings of a fancy type designed by the English cabinetmaker Thomas Sheraton; and they were introduced in this country in the early 1800s. Hitchcock types included plank (solid wood), rush, or cane seats. The back splat might be in the shape of the musical instrument the lyre, or the national emblem, an eagle. Cornucopias spilling a harvest of fruits and vegetables might be featured on slats and splats, or flowers, leaves, and fruits were stenciled against dark backgrounds and painted with powdered gold accents. Some chairs were artificially grained to resemble the elite, expensive rosewood. The top slat could have a rolled midsection to form a "pillow" shape or be wide for painting. The predominate number produced were side chairs without arms, but arm chairs were available.

Some form of the Hitchcock name often was stenciled on the back edge of the seat. Those produced from 1825-29 read "L. Hitchcock, Hitchcocks-ville, Conn. Warranted." This identification switched to "Hitchcock, Alford, & Co." during the years when a partnership existed. At its termination, the words "Lambert Hitchcock, Unionville, Conn." appeared from about 1843-1852.

Antiquers are encouraged to preserve these painted designs from the past when possible since many chairs were stripped down to their natural wood or were covered with layers of paint. Labels which help establish dates and maker identification should be saved with care and add value to pieces. If you seek an old version, look for genuine signs of wear such as rungs worn off by feet placed on them. Look for finials shaved by contact where grandpa consistently tilted his chair back against the wall. Notice legs that were roughened by being dragged or pushed out of the way when mama mopped. Naturally the color should have softened through the years, the paint worn off unevenly — more where the sitter settled against the chair than where the body didn't have contact.

*Hitchcock type pillow rail arm chair, basic black with gold grapes, melons, and leaves. 18" to seat, 18" wide at front to 15½" wide at rear, 15½" deep, 34" high.*
**$300.00 - 350.00.**

### Gothic Furniture (Circa 1820-1850s and again in the 1870s)

Gothic revival furniture is made up of bits and pieces from an old fashioned church with its carvings, spires, delicate tracery, arched windows, and steeple pointing toward the heavens. Handmade Gothic styles were popular in the 1400s and 1500s with oak the dominate wood. They were aped by Victorians who borrowed a little of this or a pinch of that from any styles they liked since their power-driven machines gave them the opportunity to zip out ornate pillars and moldings without tedious hand carving. Architecture felt the Gothic influence, especially in the structural designs of churches and schools, but furniture with this look appeared too. Pointed steeple clocks, chairs with peaks and tracery, and arched and carved case pieces mirrored Gothic, with walnut the chosen wood. Not much Gothic was made, but it did come around twice during Victoria's reign, almost introducing and closing the era.

The exuberance for copying and combining all types of furniture led to many overly ornamental styles, until some men (including England's Charles Lock Eastlake and William Morris) led a revolt because they felt inferior products were being made too rapidly and competitively by machine. Some of these leaders endorsed Gothic and patterned their "back to the basics" workmanship after the original period to produce a Neo-Gothic beginning in the 1860s in Europe and felt in the United States a few years later.

Chairs easily show a cathedral feel with peaked backs and tracery, but case pieces too included this appearance and had carvings or ornamentation of a churchy nature.

Advertisements in an 1880 catalogue for steeple clocks, available with peaks rounded or sharp, show their Gothic ancestry. Such a clock can be seen in the illustration of a china cupboard, page 69, or on page 52, photo bottom right. Thus, while Gothic was not a dominant style and not very much was made, it was around and about throughout the Victorian Era.

*Gothic type chair, oval back, hand-carved crest, 15"
to seat, 41" high. (Walnut)*
**$375.00 - 450.00.**

*Gothic type chair, demi-arms, pierced back, carved
crest, 16" to seat, 45" high. (Walnut)*
**$375.00 - 425.00.**

*(Not a true Gothic, but shows Gothic influence.)*

*Modified Gothic chair with Eastlake influ-
ence, incised carving, demi-arms, 15" to seat,
0" high. (Walnut) (Not a true Gothic, but
shows Gothic influence.)*
**$225.00 - 275.00.**

*Slant front secretary, carved pulls, molded panels, broken
pediment with applied panels and finials, Gothic arch on
upper sides, 43" wide, 21" deep, 8' 1" high. (Walnut)*
**$1,500.00 - 1,800.00.**

*Gothic type child's chair, padded arms, carved crest, 12" to
seat, 38" high. (Rosewood) (Not a true Gothic, but shows
Gothic influence.)*
**$500.00 - 575.00.**

# Chapter 4

# Curvaceous Victorian Grandeur: Louis XV Influence (Circa 1840-1865)

Louis XV was King of France from 1715 to 1774, and a style of furniture which could not seem to tolerate straight lines but appreciated rolling curves with a preference for elliptical rather than round forms was named for him. The frequent presence of marble tops attracted attention on chests, tables, dressers, commodes, or hall trees, and carved wooden pulls with nuts, grapes or other fruits appeared as if it were harvest time. Cabriole, in French, refers to a goat's leap, and the cabriole leg in furniture resembles the leg of a goat. With graceful curves it bulges at the knee, flows in and then out again at the foot. This could be enhanced with carvings, although metal mounts were common in Europe. The wood was walnut but imported rosewood and mahogany were represented along with native cherry. Victorian factories of the 1840s - 1860s liked these flowing lines, and since their new machines could copy rapidly with ease, they gleefully turned out their revised forms of Louis XV rococo by the trainloads.

The Louis XV substyle was decorative. Rococo has a picturesque sound and is derived from the French word for rock (rocailles). Throw in a lavish amount of trailing foliage and flowers, a few shells and scrolls, not perfectly balanced, and the result is elaborate ornamentation which influenced architecture as well as furniture.

Who could resist a clutter of roses, grapes, leaves, birds, rocks, shells, and various other bits of nature incorporated into carvings on chairs, tables, sofas or the like? John Belter (1795-1865) couldn't. An immigrant to the United States from Wurttemberg, Germany, where he learned his skilled trade, he advertised his wares in New York City in 1844, and wealthy clientele soon found that patronizing him was prestigious.

Solid woods split and crack when they are tortured by excessive piercing and carving, and Belter sought to use this technique. Egyptians developed a system of cutting thin wood slices to press together for durability. Laying layers alternately across the grain in order to achieve maximum strength and durability, John Belter developed the lamination process and utilized steam plus molds to bend wood as he hand carved with careful, skillful craftsmanship. His products were strong and sturdy. There is a rumor that he flung a chair out of a second story window to prove that, despite its delicate appearance, it would not shatter upon impact. It didn't. His speciality was rosewood. Copiers latched onto Belter ideas, but his interpretations remained king of the hill. When he terminated his business, he destroyed his molds and patterns to prevent possible plagiarism. Today Belter hand-carved works are priced in the thousands and receive museum status.

*Marble top parlor table, turtle top, cabriole legs, center finial at base, 33½" x 23", 28" high. (Walnut)*
**$400.00 - 500.00.**

*Gentleman's chair, finger roll, button tufted back, 15½" to seat, 40" high. (Walnut)*
**$400.00 - 450.00.**

*Serpentine carved and pierced back rail, button tufted back, Queen Anne legs, applied decorations on front apron, 5'3" outside measurement, 35" high at crest. Museum quality. (Walnut)*

Clutter, clutter everywhere, with not a space to think characterizes the Victorian taste at this time. Whatnot shelves (or if you wanted to be so Frenchy as the period was — call the fancy versions etagéres) were weighty with glass and china creations. Tables and mantles had to have elaborate vases, candleholders, and statues on them, and an impressive "centre" table was the norm, although around 1850, oval sofa tables with marble tops were becoming fashionable.

*Balloon back, finger roll side chair, hand carved crest, cabriole legs, button upholstered seat, 16" to seat, 37½" high. (Walnut)*
**$250.00 - 275.00.**

*Etegère or whatnot, fretted sides and cornice, scalloped shelves, 43" wide, 6'2" high. (Walnut)*
**$1,700.00 - 1,850.00.**

The top of the wooden frame on Louis XV chairs and sofas characteristically had a gentle concave molding now commonly termed "finger roll." This could be further adorned with carvings of fruits or leaves. If a chair back resembles a hot air balloon filled for ascension, it is termed a balloon-back, and there were many variations available.

*Lady's chair, finger roll, cabriole legs, demi-arms, 16½" to seat, 39½" high. (Walnut)*
**$350.00 - 425.00.**

*Finger roll back, cabriole legs, 4'10½" outside measurement. (Walnut)*
**$600.00 - 650.00.**

*Balloon back, finger roll side chair, horsehair seat, 17" to seat, 35½" high. (Walnut)*
**$125.00 - 150.00.**

*Balloon type back side chair, carved cresting, cabriole legs, 16½" to seat, 36" high. (Walnut)*
**$175.00 - 200.00.**

*Balloon back, finger roll side chair, demi-arms, cabriole legs, haircloth seat, 17" to seat, 36" high. (Walnut)*
**$135.00 - 160.00.**

*Modified balloon back side chair, grape and leaf crest, incised lines, veneered panels below crest, 17" to seat, 35" high. (Walnut)*
**$125.00 - 150.00.**

Upholstery left the frames exposed. While coil springs were invented in the 700s, it was not until the mid 1800s that helix springs were manufactured heaply. Louis XV substyle furniture profited from the added comfort offered. he most commonly used fabric was haircloth from the hair of the tail or mane f horses, often woven with linen. Since black predominated, many people are ot aware that various colors and small prints were available in this stiff lippery fabric. Rich satins (including satin damask), plush, brocatelle, and lain velvets (not cut velvet in patterns), plus delightfully embroidered amask were widely utilized and were frequently tied down with buttons so hat the folds made in the material formed patterns. This process is called

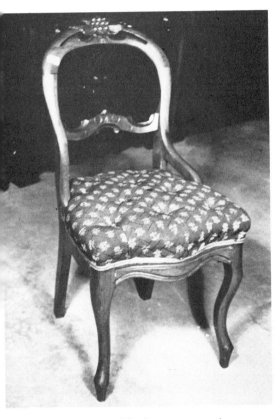

*Side chair, grape and leaf crest, serpentine apron, hip rest, Queen Anne legs, button upholstered seat, 19" to seat, 34½" high. (Walnut)*
**$145.00 - 170.00.**

*Cane chair, artificially grained.*
**$125.00 - 145.00.**

tufting. It was considered feminine to execute handwork. Young girls and women made silk patchwork or did needlepoint, embroidering in worsted and silks, for upholsterers to apply. Favorite colors included a complete range of purples, red, black, dark brown, green, soft pink, and delicate blue. Animal hair which pricked through the fabric, down, feathers, or on occasion, straw served as stuffing.

*Side chair, finger roll, tufted back, demi-arms, 18" to seat, 37" high. (Walnut)*
**$325.00 - 375.00.**

*Side chairs, oval backs, demi-arms, finger roll, tufted, original haircloth, 17" to seats, 35¼" high. (Walnut)*
**$500.00 - 600.00 pair.**

Suites were a must. Sometimes there were seven pieces to a set — a settee or sofa, arm chairs, and side chairs designed alike and covered with identical upholstery. In most bourgeois homes, the parlor was closed off, a company-only place for formal conversation when the pastor came to call, the special beau courted, or visitors of status appeared. Is it any wonder that conversation might become uncomfortably stiff to match much of the furniture?

*Gentleman's chair, finger roll, 16½" to seat, 42" high. (Walnut)*

*Lady's chair, finger roll, 16½" to seat, 40" high. (Walnut)*

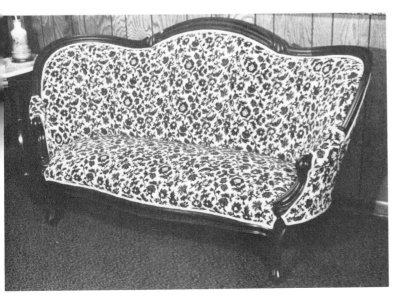

*Finger roll, 5'10" outside measurement, 38" high. (Walnut)*
**$1,750.00 - 2,000.00 the set**

With the improvement of extension tables, it was no longer necessary to pull a series of tables, some with drop leaves, together to provide additional seating in dining rooms. Side tables and chairs completed the room's furnishings.

In bedrooms, wardrobes (armoires) were convenient since closets were not built in. When clothes were not hung on wall pegs, as they were in humble dwellings, these large cupboards stored garments. Bedroom furniture included bedsteads, a dresser, and a commode to take care of personal washing needs in a time period which predated plumbing.

*Wardrobe, two large doors, two small center doors, three parallel drawers at base, brass pulls, 54" wide, 20" deep, 7'2½" high. (Walnut and burled walnut panels)*

$850.00 - 950.00.

*Dining table, oval drop leaf with three leaves, 41" x 25½", 30" high, 13" drop leaves. (Walnut)*
**$165.00 - 200.00.**

*Medallion back, carved crest with grapes and leaves, button tufted, 5'4" outside measurement. (Walnut)*
**$900.00 - 1,100.00.**

*Heart medallion back, fruit and floral carvings on three high points of back rail, cabriole legs, applied decorations on arm supports and on rolled apron, 5'6" outside measurement. (Walnut)*
**$900.00 - 1,100.00.**

43

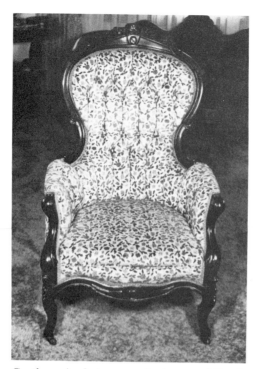

*Gentleman's chair, spoon back, carved floral crest, cabriole legs, 15" to seat, 41" high. (Rosewood frame, grained legs and apron)*
**$325.00 - 375.00.**

*Gentleman's chair, oval tufted back, open arms, cabriole legs, flower at crest, 16" to seat, 38½" high. (Walnut)*
**$475.00 - 525.00.**

*Gentleman's chair, balloon back, finger roll, open arms, button tufted back, 16" to seat, 40½" high. (Walnut)*
**$400.00 - 475.00.**

*Gentleman's chair, oval back, open arms, ha[r] carved leaf, fruit and nuts at crest, 15½" to se[e] 40" high. (Walnut)*
**$400.00 - 475.00.**

Side chair, finger roll, tufted back, demi-arms, 18" to seat, 36" high. (Walnut)
**$275.00 - 325.00.**

Side chair, demi-arms, round decorative medallion in back, ornamental crest, incised lines, 16½" to seat, 34" high. (Walnut)
**$110.00 - 135.00.**

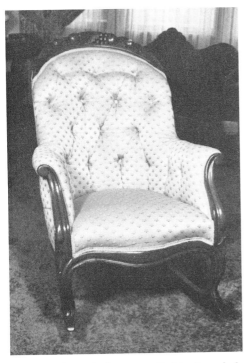

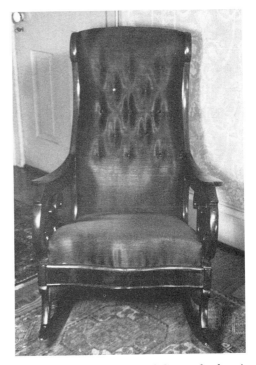

Rocking chair, fruit crest, tufted back, upholstered, closed arms, 19" to seat, 37" high. (Walnut)

**$425.00 - 475.00.**

Rocking chair, upholstered, button back, original haircloth, called Lincoln rocker, 18" to seat, 40" high. (Mahogany)
**$225.00 - 275.00.**

45

Rocking chair, upholstered, grape carved crest, applied burled panels, called Lincoln rocker, 18" to seat, 41" high. (Walnut)
**$275.00 - 300.00.**

Rocking chair, oval caned back with demi-arms, round caned seat, 16" to seat, 33" high. (Walnut)

**$175.00 - 225.00.**

Rocking chair, rectangular caned back, roll arms, U-shaped seat, Lincoln type, 17" to seat, 41" high. (Walnut and Maple)
**$185.00 - 235.00.**

Rocking chair, rectangular caned back, roll arms, square caned seat, flat front rung, 17" to seat, 39" high. (Walnut)
**$200.00 - 250.00.**

*Rocking chair, rectangular caned back, U-shaped seat, curved hoop skirt rung, sewing type rocker, 16½" to seat, 37½" high. (Walnut)*
**$185.00 - 235.00.**

*Rocking chair, child's, rectangular caned back, square seat, roll arms, flat front rung, 11" to seat, 27" high. (Walnut)*
**$200.00 - 250.00.**

*Chair, square cane seat, slat back, flat front rung, 17½" to seat, 32" high. (Walnut) Set of 4:*
**$105.00 - 120.00 each.**

*Parlor table, turtle top, molded apron, carved dog on base shelf, 23" x 36", 29" high. (Poplar and Walnut)*
**$750.00 - 825.00.**
*A solid walnut dog table would be priced near*
**$1,250.00.**

47

*Parlor table, turtle top, molded apron, finial at center of base stretchers, 30" x 21½", 26" high. (Walnut)*

**$250.00 - 300.00.**

*Parlor table, oval, molded apron, pedestal base, incised decorations, 23" x 30", 29" high. (Walnut)*

**$275.00 - 350.00.**

*Parlor table, scalloped white marble top, molded apron, cabriole legs, finial at center of base stretchers, 37" x 28", 26½" high. (Walnut)*
**$500.00 - 575.00.**

*Parlor table, oval marble top, scalloped apron with roundels, urn at base, 24" x 31", 30" high. (Walnut)*

**$525.00 - 575.00.**

48

Sewing stand, stretcher, burled drawer fronts, 21" x 16", 26" high. (Walnut)
$350.00 - 375.00.

Commode washstand, marble top, fruit carved pull, applied veneer panels on door, drawer, and stiles, 17½" x 15", 31" high, called a Somnoe in 1876 catalogue. Rare today. (Walnut)
$550.00 - 625.00.

Commode washstand, marble top, applied molding on drawer and doors, rounded corner stiles, 31" x 17", 29½" high. (Walnut)
$525.00 - 575.00.

Commode washstand, marble top with 10" splash back, incised lines on stiles, carved pulls, 37½" x 18", 29" high. (Walnut)
$650.00 - 700.00.

*Dresser, four drawers, applied panels on drawers, applied ornaments on chamfered corner stiles, 40" x 18", 39" high. (Walnut)*
**$275.00 - 300.00.**

*Commode washstand, wooden top with 6" splash back, applied circular molding on drawer and doors, projection front, applied ornaments on corner stiles, 29" x 16½", 29" high. (Walnut)*
**$375.00 - 425.00.**

*Corner whatnot, graduated shelves with fretted backs, 4'10" high. (Walnut)*
**$200.00 - 235.00.**

*Roll top secretary, knee hole base, carved pulls, 50" wide, 27" deep, 6'11" high. (Walnut)*
**$2,250.00 - 2,400.00.**

*Davenport desk, sloping lift top, fretted carved back gallery, three drawers with carved pulls, applied burled veneered panels, 25" x 20", 20½" high. (Walnut, rosewood, and grained rosewood)*

**$700.00 - 775.00.**

*Corner cupboard, one piece, chamfered stiles, 44" wide, 17" deep, 6'4½" high. (Walnut)*

**$650.00 - 750.00.**

*Corner cupboard, applied burl veneered panels and roundels, molded cornice, burl veneer panels on door inserts, 41" wide, 18½" deep, 7'10" high. (Walnut)*

**$1,400.00 - 1,600.00.**

*Bookcase, two pieces, applied ornaments, panels, chamfered stiles with applied decorations, 7'11" high. (Walnut)*

**$1,250.00 - 1,500.00.**

51

*Bedstead, circular molding on foot board, applied decorations, rolled head and foot board, 56½" wide, 72" long, 46" high. (Walnut)*
**$275.00 - 350.00.**

*Cupboard, beading, and applied ornaments on door panels, molded cornice, recessed top, 41" wide, 18" deep, 7'1" high. (Walnut)*
**$850.00 - 900.00.**

52

*Cupboard (small hutch), chamfered stiles with applied ornaments, applied circular molding on drawers, molded door frames, 30" wide, 13½" deep, 45" high. (Walnut)*
**$600.00 - 675.00.**

Bedstead, applied molding and ornaments, molded headboard rail and
molded footboard rail, 59½" wide, 82"
long, 5'1½" high. (Light wood stained
dark)

**$750.00 - 900.00.**

Dresser, marble half top, wishbone mirror, two decks
(handkerchief boxes), applied circular molding on
drawers, applied decorations on chamfered stiles,
carved pediment on mirror frame, 42" x 19", 81" high.
(Walnut and crotch mahogany veneer)

**$725.00 - 800.00.**

Dresser, marble insert, wishbone mirror, molded
burl veneer panels on drawers, applied decorations
on corner stiles, 39" x 18", 65" high. (Walnut)

**$525.00 - 575.00.**

53

*Dresser, marble insert, wishbone mirror, applied molding around drawers, applied ornaments on chamfered stiles, molded decoration on top of mirror frame, 42" wide, 19" deep, 77" high. (Walnut and crotch mahogany veneer)*
**$825.00 - 900.00.**

*Dresser, wooden top, wishbone mirror, applied molding on drawers, applied decorations on chamfered corner stiles, wooden escutcheons, fretted decoration above mirror frame, 40" x 19½", 77" high. (Walnut)*
**$525.00 - 600.00.**

*Dresser, wooden top, wishbone mirror, applied decorations on corner stiles, projection front, fret work above mirror frame, crotch mahogany veneer drawer fronts, 43½" x 19", 75" high. (Walnut, mahogany veneer)*
**$500.00 - 550.00**

*Lift top commode, one drawer, three simulated drawers, applied decorations on chamfered corner stiles, 33½" x 18½", 33½" high. (Walnut)*

**$350.00 - 425.00.**

*Dresser, wooden top, circular ring molding on drawers, carved drawer pulls, rounded corner stiles, boxes or decks are missing, 28" x 12", 26½" high. (Walnut)*

**$350.00 - 425.00.**

# Chapter 5

# The Renaissance Extravaganza (Circa 1850-1885)

Renaissance. This rich sounding name represents the revival or rebirth of learning and art which occurred in Europe in the fourteenth, fifteenth, and sixteenth centuries and shows characteristics of that era. It was a time when the Roman and Greek cultures were being revived. Since Victorians were eclectic (copied and combined what they liked from previous periods) Renaissance characteristics appealed to furniture makers, although one authority who explored the industry in Grand Rapids, Michigan, claimed, "It is doubtful that any extensive research into period styles lay behind the production of pieces so designated."

High, high, high might have been the theme song during the 1870s. Elaborate molding featuring decorative crests and pediments produced heavy, imposing pieces including tall massive bedsteads, sideboards, and secretary desks. There is nothing shy or shrinking about Renaissance pieces. They are bold and generous in design and were prevalent from about 1850 through 1885. Their excessive craving for walnut must have made conservationalists shriek, "You're paranoid," as they realized that several normal size beds could be created from one wood-devouring Renaissance giant. Actually, walnut forests were becoming depleted by 1880 so there was cause for concern, but customers must be served.

Wood carvers emigrated from the shipyards in Glasgow, Scotland, and, since they were trained to carve ship figureheads, it was no trouble at all to transfer their talents to adorning furniture elaborately. Many contributed their skills to Grand Rapids companies and undoubtedly were pleased when their craftmanship was acknowledged since furniture at fairs was tagged as carved, designed, or finished by the particular person named. Therefore, although much was machine done, handwork enhanced expensive offerings from high quality factories such as Berkey and Gay, the first firm to advertise on a national scale; Nelson Matter; the Widdicombs; C.C. Comstock; the Phoenix Furniture Company; and others. Many furniture factories in other locales probably employed Scottish immigrants and profited from their creative skills.

Grand Rapids companies' firsts show ingenuity; that was one reason its industry prospered.

1836 — "Deacon" William Haldene, father of Grand Rapids Furniture, handcrafted the first commercial products in his home.

1858 — the railroad came to town. Prior to that, during warm weather there was steamship travel from 1837 on, but not when winter's freezing cold came and blocked waterways with ice. Overland travel was difficult. A plank road from Kalaazoo was constructed from 1852-1855. The logs dug into the ground at regular intervals helped prevent the formation of ruts and kept

*Sideboard, white marble top, round sunken panels in base with nuts and grape carving, chamfered stiles with applied decoration, top with two oval mirrors, central roundel, crest with leaf and nuts. 54" wide, 19½" deep, 6'4" high. (Walnut)*
**$1,650.00 - 1,750.00.**

*Bedstead, sunken double panel on headboard, molded footboard with applied decoration, carved pediment and urn finials on headboard, 62" wide, 70" long, 7' high. (Walnut)*
**$1,500.00 - 1,750.00.**

carriage or wagon wheels from submerging in mud during wet weather.

About 1858 — salesmen or the manufacturer journeyed by rail from town to town showing sketches of merchandise available and selling from a loaded freight car or taking orders. Full scale examples or small models, which were referred to as salesmen's samples, could be displayed. When Elias Matter took new fangled photographs of furniture in 1862, it became obsolete to carry replicas, and catalogues evolved.

1850-1870s — furniture displays at local merchandise fairs grew into grandiose shows.

1861 — C.C. Comstock decided to establish a "wareroom" at Peoria, Illinois, expanding later to include St. Louis, Missouri. There merchandise could be displayed and sold.

This was a great age of industrial experimentation and expansion as this country began to switch from agriculture to industry, and a middle class which could afford to purchase mass produced items began to emerge. Meanwhile, the wealthy sought to outdo each other, and what better way could they flaunt their riches than through conspicuous homes, furnishings, and lavish entertaining? This Gilded Age undoubtedly helped bring forth the extravagant Renaissance style. Marble tops and naturalistic carvings remained in favor as wood carvers went chisel happy, each pediment seemingly meant to show off their skills, while hand carved fruit, nuts, and leaves continued to

*Bedstead, veneer panels, roundels, carved and applied decorations including a head of Columbia in the elaborate crest, urn finials, 60" wide, 81" long, 8'2" high. (Walnut)*
**$2,500.00 - 2,750.00.**

serve as pulls on drawers. Roundels and rounded moldings remained popular. Dressing case mirrors were huge.

An award-winning extravaganza at the Centennial Exposition in Philadelphia, Pennsylvania, in 1876 at the nation's one hundredth happy birthday party must have shouted, "Look at me!" It was something to see. Nelson, Matter & Company vehemently denied their exotic bed was designed for this specific event. They maintained it was a bedstead they took from the company stock room. Niches on the frame contained statuettes with George Washington presiding over the middle of the headboard and Columbia, a carving of a woman representing the United States of America, at center stage on the foot of the bed. Columbus and Guttenberg were present and at least five more figures filled their own niches. Surmounting all was a wooden eagle with his wings spread wide, ready to swoop down to pounce on his prey. This wondrous creation sold for three thousand dollars at the fair and has since disappeared. Run quickly and inspect grandma's attic. It may be lurking in your ancestral garret and if found could startle and arouse patriotic fervor in this generation also.

All of the furniture created during the latter Renaissance years did not strictly adhere to the characteristics of this age. Some Eastlake influences were beginning to be seen. This is dramatically demonstrated when one compares two catalogues from Nelson, Matter & Co. In the 1873 catalogue rounded arches were in evidence, and, merely three years later, in the 1876 catalogue, the straight line feel began to appear. This squaring off of details and addition of incised decorative lines will be obvious in some of the Renaissance pieces that are pictured at the conclusion of this chapter.

*Commode, white marble top, unusual turned gallery with roundels, pendent pulls with brass backplates, raised veneer panels on doors. 31" wide, 16" deep, 40½" high. (Walnut)*

*Dresser, white marble top, pagoda cornice shows Oriental influence, carved pediment, roundels, pendent pulls with brass backplates, slipper drawer in base resembles apron (called secret drawer by some), (Walnut) 46" wide, 20" deep, 7'6½" high.*

*Bracket caster for bedstead*

*Bedstead, pagoda cornice shows Oriental influence, carved pediment, veneer panels on both head and foot board, heavy duty 2" porcelain casters are on applied 6" brackets, side rails have burl panels, 58" wide, lengthened to 88" long, 7'7" high. (Walnut).*

**$2,500 - 3,100.00 the set.**

*Dresser, burl veneer panels on drawers, stiles, and mirror frame, marble insert, carved pediment, roundels, ebony and gilt drops (now called tear drop pulls) 39" wide x 17½" deep, 6'4" high. (Walnut).*

**$475.00 - 525.00.**

*Dresser with decks, white marble insert, veneer panels on drawers, decks, and mirror frame, carved pulls, scalloped apron, roundels, carved pediment, 39" wide, 19" deep, 6'10½" high. (Walnut)*

**$600.00 - 650.00.**

*Dressing case, white marble on two decks and top, burl veneer panels on drawers, ebony and gilt drop pulls (tear drops), chamfered stiles, veneer panels on mirror frame, carved pediment, 56" wide, 22" deep, 8'1" high. (Walnut)*

**$1,200.00 - 1,500.00.**

*Dresser with boxes, white marble top, round and oval molding on drawers, unfolding oak leaf pulls, pierced carved pediment, 40" wide, 18" deep, 6'6½" high, May 21, 1863 stamped on back of each pull. (Walnut)*

**$575.00 - 650.00.**

61

Dresser, two decks, wooden top, burl veneer panels on drawers, roundels, ebony and gilt pulls (tear drop), fret work and carved pediment on mirror frame, 40" wide, 18" deep, 5'11" high, Eastlake influence. (Walnut) $425.00 - 475.00.

Dressing case, white marble on decks and top, veneer panels on drawers and mirror frame, pulls have been replaced, carved pediment has small piece missing, 44" wide 20" deep, 7'3¼" high. (Eastlake influence). (Walnut)

$425.00 - 525.00.

Commode washstand, wooden top with splash back, candle or soap stands, veener panels on drawer and doors, tear drop pulls, 30" wide, 16" deep, 39" high. (Walnut)
$375.00 - 425.00.

Commode washstand, somnoe, white marble top, chamfered pillar stiles, veneered and molded drawer and door, rare, 21 wide, 17 deep, 32" high. (Walnut)
**$650.00 - 700.00.**

Sideboard, marble top, fruit carvings in sunken panels on door, sunken panels on drawers, teardrops, chamfered, beveled mirror, pediment with pierced carving, some pieces missing, 52" wide, 24" deep, 7'11" high, (Walnut)
**$900.00 - 1,100 as is, $2,000.00 - 2,200.00 restored.**

Sideboard, white marble top, elaborate fish and fowl carvings on three flush molded panels, carved pediment, shelves and molding on mirror frame, 47½" wide, 19" deep, 7'9" high. (Walnut)
**$2,200.00 - 2,350.00.**

Sideboard, white marble top, molded flush panels with bulging carved fruit, carved pulls on molded drawers, applied decorations and shelves on mirror frame, roundels, carved pediment, 52" wide 19" deep, 7'8" high. (Chestnut)  **$2,600.00 - 2,750.00.**

63

*Arm chair, Eastlake influence, burled panels, incised carving, roundels, carved crest, tufted back. (Walnut)*

*Side chair, Eastlake influence, burled panels, incised carving, roundels, carved crest, tufted back. (Walnut)*

*Double framed back shows Eastlake influence, burled panels, incised carving, tufted back and arms, roundels, carved crest, 4'6½", outside measurement. (Walnut)*

**$1,300.00 - 1,500.00 the set**

*Double framed back, Eastlake influence, tufted back, roundels, veneer panels, carved crest, 6'1" outside measurement, (Walnut)*
**$2,000.00 - 2,500.00.**

*Bedstead, veneer panels, oval molding, center roundel, urn finials, pediment has pierced and ornate carving, 55" wide, 82" long, 6'2" high, (Walnut)*

**$700.00 - 850.00.**

*Bedstead, applied carved plaque in center of headboard, urn finials, roundels, carved pediment, 53½" wide, 82" long as lengthened, 7'5" high. (Walnut)*
**$850.00 - 1,000.00.**

65

Bedstead, applied fruits on head and foot boards, molding, three sunken arched panels on headboard, urn finials, ornately carved pediment, 57″ wide, 79″ long, 6′5″ high. (Walnut)
$1,350.00 - 1,500.00.

Side chair, Eastlake influence, veneer panels, incised carving, carved crest. (Walnut)
$210.00 - 235.00.

Side chair, needlepoint seat, only two turned rungs, pierced and carved splat, roundels carved crest. (Walnut)
$200.00 - 235.00.

*lant front secretary, veneer panels, ebony and
It pulls (tear drop), broken carved pediment,
5" wide, 22" deep, 8'3" high. (Walnut)*
**$1,200.00 - 1,350.00.**

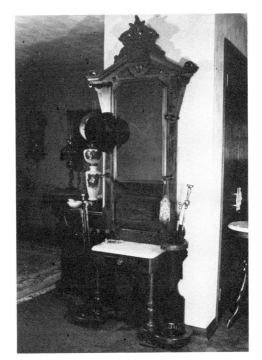

*Hall tree, white marble over drawer, veneer
panels, roundels, carved pediment, 19½" wide,
10½" deep, 7'5½" high. (Walnut)*
**$950.00 - 1,050.00.**

*Iall tree, arched mirror, open carving, broken
ediment, one leg is thicker than the other
ndicating hand carving, 6'7" high. (Walnut)*
**$600.00 - 675.00.**

*Hall tree with arched mirror, one drawer with
carved pull, open carving, molded pediment,
7'2" high. (Walnut)*
**$675.00 - 750.00.**

*Dining table, round extension, pedestal base, applied burl panels, roundels, five leaves. 45½" diameter. (Walnut)*
**$1,100.00 - 1,250.00.**

*Parlor table, oval wooden top, molded apron, pedestal base with applied roundels, 29" x 22". (Walnut)*

**$350.00 - 375.00.**

*Parlor table, oval white marble top, pendent finials, roundels, scalloped apron, 29" x 23". (Walnut)*

**$475.00 - 550.00.**

*Parlor table, oval white marble top, carved legs with central finial, 29" x 34". (Walnut)*
**$675.00 - 725.00.**

*China cupboard, veneer molded panels on doors, drawers, and cornice, carved pediment, unusual brass handles, roundels, 45" wide, 18" deep, 8'3" high. (Walnut)*

**$1,700.00 - 1,850.00.**

*Cylinder desk, comes in four parts so that top and base may be used separately, applied panels and roundels, veneer on rolled surface, carved pediments, two paneled doors at base, 68½" wide, 25" deep, 11'11" high. Museum quality. (Walnut)*

69

Cane chair, splat back with veneer panels, incised carving. Applied veneer heart in middle of crest. Chair was made in the late 1800s as an engagement gift. Demi-arms, (Walnut). Set of four: **$115.00 - 125.00 each.**

Cane chair, splat back with veneer vase and incised leaves, incised crest, round seat, Demi-arms. (Walnut). Set of four: **$115.00 - 125.00 each.**

Arm chair, applied roundels in center and sides, burl panels, crest with leaves, (Walnut) **$250.00 - 300.00.**

Arm chair, veneer panels, roundels, carved crest, (Walnut) **$300.00 - 350.00.**

# Chapter 6
# The Misfits — Furniture That Does Not Categorically Fit Into Any Substyle

During the Victorian period countless pieces of furniture were made that do not strictly classify as Empire, Louis XV, Renaissance, Gothic, or Eastlake. Cane chairs, for example, were made by the millions from 1840 through the 1890s and do not meet the structural characteristics of the various Victorian substyles. The same holds true of work tables, many parlor tables, common washstands, and the ordinary furniture pieces. For lack of a name, these could make up the miscellany and numerically they embody as many articles as any of the other styles.

*Cane chair, round seat, slat back, Demi-arms, thousands and thousands ade from mid-until late 1800s, (Walnut), Set of four:*
**$95.00 - 110.00 each.**

Picture a common washstand as a table with a back rail, one drawer with round knob pull, four legs, and a bottom shelf. Its turned legs do not suggest an individual influence such as cabriole legs do — namely Louis XV. There is no place to imitate the tracery of a church window for a Gothic feel. How could a small piece terminate with a bold crest as most Renaissance types do? Without incised lines, especially railroad tracks, who's to say it's Eastlake? This makes classifying it and pushing it into one time zone slightly difficult. Because of this, Chapter Six presents furniture which could fit in almost any place, and pictures stereotyped objects which were made repetitiously year after year in almost the exact pattern and manner.

*Common washstand, spool turned towel bars, top 20″ wide, 15½″ deep, (Walnut)*
**$200.00 - 225.00.**

*Marble top parlor table, turtle top, veneer panels, roundels, 31" x 20½", 30½" high. (Walnut)*

**$475.00 - 525.00.**

*Marble top parlor table, rectangular, veneered apron, 20½" x 16½", 29" high. (Walnut)*

**$375.00 - 400.00.**

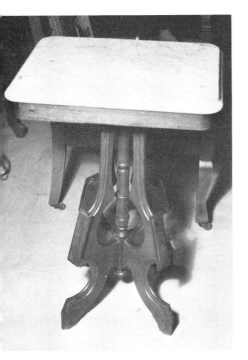

*Marble top parlor table, rectangular, pedestal base with unusual rectangular burl veneer panels on legs, 20" x 16", 28½" high. (Walnut)*

**$375.00 - 400.00.**

*Marble top parlor table, oval, carved apron, burl veneer, 32" x 24", 29" high. (Walnut)*

**$550.00 - 650.00.**

*Tilt top table, scalloped legs, tripod base, 32½"*
*diameter. (Walnut)*
**$350.00 - 400.00.**

*Parlor table, oval, deep apron, four legs, family*
*piece probably handmade as top is on crooked,*
*29" x 21", 27" high. (Walnut)*
**$115.00 - 145.00.**

*Parlor table, oval, molded apron, incised carv-*
*ing, 32" x 24", 29½" high. (Walnut)*
**$300.00 - 350.00.**

*Parlor table, oval, molded apron, pedestal base*
*with incised lines, 31½" x 23½", 29" high.*
*(Walnut)*
**$300.00 - 350.00.**

*Parlor table, round, tripod base with middle finial, molded apron, 29" diameter, 27" high. (Walnut)*
**$350.00 - 400.00.**

*Lamp stand, incised lines on pedestal, 14½" diameter, 32" high. (Walnut)*
**$110.00 - 135.00.**

*Parlor table, oval, molded apron, pedestal base, 37" x 28", 30" high. (Walnut)*
**$350.00 - 400.00.**

*Lamp stand, pedestal base with incised lines, 14" diameter, 31" high. (Walnut)*
**$110.00 - 135.00.**

*Lamp stand, white marble top, round buttons on base, pillar with four branches at top and bottom. (Walnut)*
**$225.00 - 250.00.**

*Commode washstand, marble top and splash back with soap or candle shelves, veneer panels, roundels, ebony and gilt pulls (tear drops), central roundel on drawer, 30" wide, 16" deep, 37" high. (Walnut)*
**$650.00 - 700.00.**

*Lamp stand, white marble top, roundels on pedestal base. (Walnut)*
**$275.00 - $350.00.**

*Bureau washstand, marble top and splash back, beading on drawers, round knobs, 29" wide, 14" deep, 39½" high. (Walnut)*
**$500.00 - $550.00.**

Commode washstand, marble top and splash back with soap or candle stands, retractable towel rod, circle molded flush panels on doors, 30" wide, 15½" deep, 37½" high. (Walnut)
**$575.00 - 625.00.**

Commode washstand, unusual carved handles, chamfer stiles with applied decorations, molded drawer and doors, back splash, 30" wide, 17" deep, 36" high. (Walnut)
**$375.00 - 425.00.**

Lift top commode washstand, paneled doors, right drawer fake, round pulls, 36½" wide, 18½" deep, 35" high. (Walnut)
**$350.00 - 400.00.**

Commode washstand, top and drawer serpentine, two wooden knobs, fine dovetails, applied turnings on stiles. (Mahogany veneer drawer, top walnut, rest stained walnut)
**$275.00 - 350.00.**

*Bureau washstand with splash back and towel bar ends, projection front, round knobs, chamfer stiles, plank sides, 37" wide, 15½" deep, 35¼" high. (Walnut)*
**$375.00 - 450.00.**

*Bureau washstand with two rectractable towel bars, mushroom handles, applied decoration on stiles, oval molding on drawers, projection front, 29½" wide x 15½" deep, 30½" high. (Walnut)*
**$325.00 - 375.00.**

*Bureau washstand, raised panels, applied decorations on stiles, plain spalsh back, 29" wide, 15½" deep, 36" high. (Walnut)*
**$250.00 - 325.00.**

Dresser, uncluttered lines, round
wooden pulls, top one piece of
wood, 40" wide, 18" deep, 37"
high. (Walnut)
**$225.00 - 275.00.**

Cane chair, upholstered with needlepoint, burl
veneer on top slat, demi arms, 17" to seat, 33" high.
(Walnut)

**$95.00 - 110.00.**

Bureau washstand, splash back, round knob pulls,
scalloped apron, 29" wide x 14" deep, 35" high.
(Poplar, Stained Walnut)
**$250.00 - 325.00.**

*Cane chair, square seat, two curved slats, 17"
to seat, 31½" high. (Walnut) Set of four:*
**$95.00 - 110.00 each.**

*Cane seat and back chair, oval back panel,
round seat, rectangular rung, 17½" to seat, 32"
high. (Walnut) Set of four:*
**$115.00 - 135.00 each**

*Cane seat, three slats, carved crest, incised
lines, demi-arms, 17" to seat, 34" high. (Walnut) Set of four:*
**$105.00 - 115.00 each.**

*Cane seat and back arm chair, arms extend
about half way, 19½" to seat, 39" high.
(Walnut)*

**$125.00 - 145.00.**

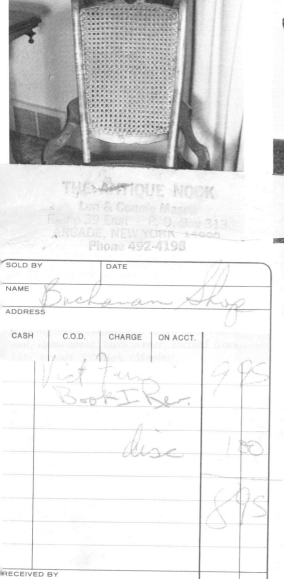

...king chair, tufted, incised lines, 15" to seat, 29½"
...h. (Walnut)

**$225.00 - 275.00.**

Child's rocking chair, rectangular back, U-
shaped seat, rolled arms, 26" high. (Maple)
**$145.00 - 170.00.**
(23-strand graduated sleigh bells.
**$250.00.**
Brass kettle, 12" diameter, 8" tall.
**$95.00.**

*Drop leaf sewing stand, leaves have scalloped edges, square legs, raised panels, round knobs on drawers, top 18" x 24", 29" high, 11½" drops. (Walnut)*

**$350.00 - 375.00.**

*Shaving stand, serpentine rectangular white marble top, serpentine drawer and sides, pedestal base, swing mirror in wishbone frame. Rare. (Walnut)*

**$900.00 - 1,000.00.**

*Work table, square legs, top 21½" x 16½", 29" high. (Walnut)*

**$150.00 - 175.00.**

*Work table, scalloped top, wooden knobs, top 32" x 19", 29" high. (Walnut)*
**$175.00 - 200.00.**

*Drop leaf sewing stand, leaves cut off slightly, top 18¼ x 18", 28½" high, leaves were 9" but now are 7". (Cherry with tiger maple drawer fronts)*
**$275.00 - 350.00.**

*Lamp table, round pull, top 20" x 17½, 26½" high. (Cherry with poplar drawer front)*
**$175.00 - 200.00.**

Cylinder front secretary, comes in three sections: secretary top, roll top and two drawers, base drawers and cupboard. Old wavy glass, burl veneer panels, brass centers on round pulls, cornice with applied decoration, 37" wide, 24" deep, 7'7" high. (Walnut)

$1,400.00 - 1,600.00.

Cylinder front secretary, rounded drawer, incised carving, burl veneer, bale handles have acorn and leaf back plates, 32" wide, 21" deep, 6'8" high. (Walnut)

$1,500.00 - 1,750.00.

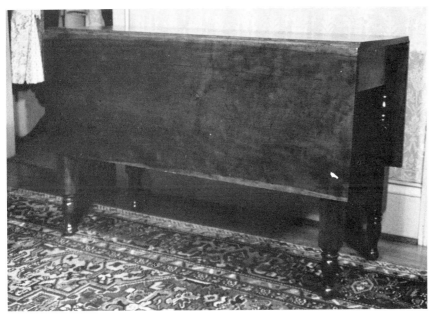

*Dining table, rectangular drop leaf, square turned legs, wooden slides. Top and drops are each one board, 44" wide, 18" deep, 28½" high, drops 15½". (Cherry)*
**$275.00 - 325.00.**

*Cupboard, four drawers, two paneled doors, wooden knobs, ivory escutcheons, shelf on top gallery, hand done, 43" wide, 19" deep, 5'6" high. (Walnut)*
**$1,300.00 - 1,400.00.**

*Cupboard, paneled doors, plank sides, rounded stiles, dovetailed drawers, planed inside door, six panes of glass separated by muntins, two pieces, china cupboard top, 65" wide x 19½" deep base, 7'7" high. (Walnut)*
**$2,250.00 - 2,500.00.**

Dining table, oval drop leaf, extension, 26" x 40", 14½" drops. (Walnut)
**$165.00 - 195.00.**

Single drop leaf table, scalloped bottom shelf, rounded ends on single drop, finished back, square legs, 41" x 22½", 29½ high, single leaf 14½". (Walnut)
**$375.00 - 450.00.**

Cupboard, paneled doors, molded drawers at base, double arched glass china cupboard top, plank sides, 49" wide, 18" deep, 7'7" tall. (Walnut)
**$1,200.00 - 1,300.00.**

Common washstand, towel bar ends, curved splash back, 26" x 15", 33" high. (Walnut) $190.00 - 225.00.

Dining table, drop leaf extension, seven leaves, 26" x 42", 12" drops. (Walnut) $250.00 - 300.00.

Common washstand, splash back and towel bar ends, 22½" x 15½", 33½" high. (Stained walnut, three oak legs, one pine) $125.00 - 135.00.

Common washstand, splash back resembles a broken pediment, roundel, carved pulls on drawer, towel bar ends, 29" x 15½", 28" high. (Walnut) $225.00 - 275.00.

## Chapter 7
## Eastlake Goes Straight (Circa 1870-1890)

Straight box-like furniture is stronger than that which is unnaturally curved; it is pleasing to behold, and an additional advantage is that simple structural lines do not waste wood. These were theories expressed by the English furniture designer Charles Lock(e) Eastlake who wrote a book, *Hints on Household Taste,* which was published around 1868. It did not take too many years for his ideas to float across the Atlantic and to penetrate the heads of American manufacturers. Grand Rapids, Michigan, began to express Eastlake sentiments as the 1870s terminated, and other factories elsewhere felt the Eastlake tidal wave also. Charles Lock wanted designers, and factories began to hire professionals to plan their products.

*Commode washstand, mirror top, brass bail handles on drawers, incised lines, dark marble top, 30" x 16", 70" high. (Walnut)*
**$450.00 - 500.00.**

Eastlake and some of his cohorts felt that machines encouraged the marketing of speedily made inferior merchandise produced by workmen whose skills were in danger of deteriorating. He deplored the sham and pretense of irregular or curved lines plus ornate ornamentation and sought a return to basic straight lines. Forget competition which cheapened the industry's output. Designers on this side of the Atlantic Ocean heard his message and responded by adopting rectilinear lines. The only difficulty was, they were used to being able to create curlicues with easy machine work so they took Eastlake rectangles (some with Gothic decorations and feel; some inspired by Japan's clean functional lines) and zealously applied ornamentation and appendages.

In England, oak and ash were utilized frequently, but in the United States, walnut clung around with much cherry (or maple stained dark) prevalent. Chip carving and incised lines became the norm. Currently, when antiquers note that parallel lines are inscribed in wood, they refer to them as "railroad tracks" and immediately think late 1800s . . . Eastlake. Thus, even if Charles Lock Eastlake's sermons on clean lines were ignored, his preaching regarding strong furniture won converts who began to turn out merchandise with a sturdy squarish or rectangular appearance. Who can blame workmen who enjoyed going creative? Besides, it must have been difficult to quell quickly

Chiffonier, six full drawers, hinged stile locks all drawers when closed, incised lines, flower in center of each drawer, top pierced rail with deck, brass bail pulls, roundels, 40″ wide, 19″ deep, 66″ high. (Walnut)

$1,050.00 - 1,150.00.

Dressing case with white marble top on decks and top, ebony and gilt pulls (tear drops), applied panel decorations, two large drawers with machined dovetails, carved pediment with incised lines, 41″ wide, 17½″ deep, 6′10″ high. (Walnut)

$650.00 - 750.00.

the extravagance of Renaissance renditions. Among the following pictures that have been classified as Eastlake, many Renaissance features are in evidence. One sometimes reaches a point as to whether to call a piece "Eastlake with Renaissance influence" or "Renaissance with Eastlake influence." The final determination must, of course, be which features are more dominant in the article being described.

*Chiffonier, five drawers, hinged stile locks all drawers when closed, burl veneer, incised flower decoration and lines, applied decoration on stile, peg machined dovetails on drawers, 36" wide, 20" deep, 47" high. (Walnut)*

**$400.00 - 500.00.**

*Dresser with decks, white marble insert, carved pulls on drawer panels, roundels, panel sides, carved pediment, 40" wide, 19" deep, 7'1" high. (Walnut)*
**$475.00 - 525.00.**

Dresser, dark marble top, brass bail handles, railroad incised lines, machine dovetails, burl veneer on drawers, 38¼" wide, 18" deep, 30¼" high. (Walnut)
**$250.00 - 300.00.**

Bureau washstand, burl veneer panels on stiles, incised railroad track lines, scalloped splash back, brass drop pulls, 30" wide, 16" deep, 30" high. (Walnut)
**$300.00 - 350.00.**

Chiffonier, six drawers with brass drop pulls, incised carving on stiles, applied leaves and flower decorations on beveled mirror frame, gargoyle heads, 38" wide, 17" deep, 70" high. (Walnut)
**$800.00 - 850.00.**

Commode washstand, retractable towel bar, incised decorations and railroad track lines, white marble top and splash back with candle or soap stands, projection top drawer, 31" wide, 15½" deep, 33" high. (Walnut)
$600.00 - 650.00.

Bedstead, burl panels, incised lines, leaf carvings, roundels, 54" wide, 75" long, 6'5" high. (Walnut)
$525.00 - 625.00.

Bedstead, burl veneer panels, garland carving, incised lines, carved flat cornice, 59½" wide, 75" long, 6'1" high. (Walnut)

$575.00 - 675.00.

Bedstead, crotch veneer panels, incised lines, chip carving, three rectangular panels, 58" wide, 79" long, 6'6" high. (Walnut)
$700.00 - 800.00.

Bedstead, veneer panels, pierced and incised carving, carved pediment, 60" wide, 76" long, 7'4" high.

$2,500.00 - 2,800.00 the set.

Commode washstand, white marble top with candle or soap stands on splash back, burl veneer and incised carving on doors and drawer, applied leaf on stiles, panel sides, 28½" wide, 15½ deep, 32½" high.

Dresser, white marble top, veneer panels, mirror, incised carving, carved pediment, 50" wide, 21½" deep, 7'4½" high. Renaissance influence. (Walnut)

93

*Bedstead, carved garlands on cornice, burl veneer panels, sunken molded velvet covered panel in head board, pierced carving on foot board, 60" wide, 81" long, 7'1" high. (Walnut)*
**$850.00 - 950.00.**

*Sideboard, white marble top, ebony and gilt pulls (tear drops) on parallel drawers, two doors with veneer panels, pierced and incised carving, pediment, shelf above mirror, 41" wide, 18" deep, 7' high. (Walnut)*
**$1,100.00 - 1,300.00.**

*Cylinder secretary, burl veneer on rolled front, brass bail handles on drawers, pull out writing surface, cornice has chip and incised carving, 36" wide, 22" deep, 7'5" high. (Walnut)*
**$1,300.00 - 1,500.00.**

*Cupboard and server, two pieces, pegged top has glass doors, cornice, paneled base doors, incised railroad track lines, 44" wide, 19" deep at base, 7'2½" high. (Walnut fronts, sides are poplar stained walnut)*
**$750.00 - 900.00.**

Slant front secretary, burl veneer panels, cornice, panel sides, two sections, 37¼" wide, 17" deep, 6'5" high. (Walnut front, sides base wood stained walnut)

$1,300.00 - 1,400.00.

Chiffonier with attached cheval mirror, incised lines, brass bail pulls, hinged stile locks all six drawers when closed, carved cornice, 59" wide, 18½" deep, 6'5" high. (Walnut)

$850.00 - 925.00.

Lift lid schoolmaster's desk, two pieces, leather insert on slanting top, plain gallery, incised railroad lines, burl veneer, 28½" wide, 25" deep, 33" high. (Walnut)

$475.00 - 525.00.

Lift lid kneehole desk with trestle base, burl veneer on drawers, brass bail handles, 38" wide, 27½" deep, 33" high. (Walnut)

$650.00 - 725.00.

95

*Hall tree, garlands and applied pillars, incised lines, pierced carving, carved pediment, drawer with marble shelf, 40" wide, 14" deep, 6'2½" high. Renaissance influence. (Walnut)*
**$900.00 - 1,000.00.**

*Pier mirror, white marble shelf, pilaster and veneer panels, incised lines, carved pediment. Eastlake with Renaisance influence, 25" wide, 19½" deep, 8'10" high. (Walnut)*
**$750.00 - 900.00.**

*Mirror, pilasters, incised lines, chip carving on cornice, 22" wide, 4'7½" high. (Walnut)*
**$150.00 - 175.00.**

*Pier mirror with dark marble slab, applied pilasters, incised flower carving, cornice, 26½" wide, 12" deep, 7'4" high. (Walnut)*
**$575.00 - 650.00.**

*Parlor table, rectangular, burl veneer, roundels, legs joined by central turned stretcher, 30" x 21½", 28" high. Eastlake with Renaissance influence. (Walnut)*
**$275.00 - 325.00.**

*Victorian room scene. Tilt top table is period piece. Pair of gentleman's chairs, oval tufted back, cabriole legs, flower crest, 16" to seat, 38½" high. (Walnut)*
**$475.00 - 525.00 each.**

97

*Bureau washstand with splash back and towel bar ends, projection front, round knobs, chamfer stiles, plank sides, 37" wide, 15½" deep, 35¼" high. (Walnut)*   **$375.00 - 450.00.**

*Music box, Symphonian, patented 1889, stand beneath has drawer for 10½" tune sheets, 18¼" wide, 14½" deep, 12" high. (Mahogany veneer)*   **$2,500.00 - 2,700.00.**

Parlor table, scalloped white marble top, molded apron, cabriole legs, finial at center of base stretchers, 37" x 26", 26½" high. (Walnut)
**$500.00 - 575.00.**

Eclectic sofa, Egyptian lady head from Empire, leg style Louis XIV, round tufted back, Louis XV, Renaissance cresting, incised carving on apron Eastlake, five piece set.
**$6,000.00 - 6,500.00.**

*Bedstead from painted cottage suit, soft blue panels with flowers, leaves, and crane on head and foot board. Back stamp reads "J.H. Crane's Furniture Warerooms, S.E. corner of 4th St. and Washington Ave., St. Louis, Mo.," 57½" wide, 72" rails, 6'1" high. (Pine)*

*Commode washstand from painted cottage suit, artificial graining with painted daisies, brass bail handles, 29" wide, 15" deep, 35" high. (Pine) Four piece set:*
**$1,500.00 - 1,750.00.**

*Commode washstand from painted cottage suit, gray background, blue panels with flowers, 29½" wide, 15½" deep, 32½" high. (Pine) Four piece set:*
**$1,500.00 - 1,750.00.**

*Victorian room scene. Side chair, oval back, demi-arms, finger roll, tufted, original hair-cloth, 17" to seat, 35¼" high. (Walnut)*
**$250.00 - 300.00.**

*Commode washstand, chamfer stiles with applied decoration, veneered molded panels on doors and drawer, molded sides, ebony and gilt pulls (tear drops), small size, 29" wide, 16½" deep, 26½" high. (Walnut)*
**$275.00 - 325.00.**

*Empire room scene. Empire transitional sofa, fruit cresting, serpentine rail, applied decorations, button tied back, 6'3" outside measurement. (Walnut and mahogany veneer)*
**$900.00 - 1,100.00.**

*Empire oval parlor table, lyre type base, beading, 35" x 22½", 28" high. (Mahogany and mahogany veneer)*
**$400.00 - 450.00.**

*Victorian room scene. Slant front secretary, burl veneer panels, cornice, panel sides, 37½"
wide, 17" deep, 6'5" high. (Walnut front, sides base wood stained walnut)*   **$1,300.00 - 1,400.00.**
*Gentleman's chair, carved floral crest, cabriole legs, 15" to seat, 41" high. (Rosewood
frame, grained leg and apron)*                                              **$325.00 - 375.00.**

Victorian room scene. Marble top parlor table, turtle top, c riole legs with leaf carvings, 33½" x 23", 28" high. (Walnu $400.00 - 500.00.

Louis XV Renaissance side chair with Eastlake influence. cised carving, veneer panels, roundels, pierced splat back a crest. (Walnut)    $200.00 - 235.

Cylinder secretary, burl veneer on rolled front, brass bail handles, pull out writing surface, cornice has chip and incised carving, 36" wide, 22" deep, 7'5" high. (Walnut)
$1,300.00 - 1,500.00.

Commode washstand, marble top and splash back with soap or candle shelves, veneer panels, roundels, ebony and gilt pulls (tear drops), central roundel on drawer, 30" wide, 16" deep, 37" high. (Walnut)
$650.00 - 700.00.

Pierced carved back separates two panel back, incised carving,, molded crest, 4'10" outside measurement, 41" high.

**$1,100 - 1,400 the set.**

*Platform rocker, incised carving, pierced carving on crest, 37½" high.*

*Arm chair, incised carving, pierced carving on crest, 45" high. (Walnut)*

105

*Mirror frame back is tufted, tufted arms, burl veneer on crest, roundels, 4'10½" outside measurement, 43" high. (Walnut)*

**$600.00 - 650.00.**

*Side chair, incised lines, demi-arms, carved crest, 38" high. (Walnut)*

**$125.00 - 145.00.**

*Arm chair, incised carving, burl veneer carved crest, 41½" high. (Walnut)*

**$175.00 - 200.00.**

ouble frame back, tufted, pierced carving, incised carving, carved crest, burl veneer, 4'11"
utside measurement, 41½" high. (Walnut)

**$650.00 - 750.00.**

ane chair, square seat and back, turned rail
top, demi-arms, 38" high. (Walnut) Set of
our:

**$135.00 - 150.00 each.**

Youth chair, cane seat, top turned rung flat-
tened from feet rubbing across it, incised lines,
unusual because of birds and garland inlay
work on the top slat, 21" to seat, 35" high.
(Walnut)

**$175.00 - 200.00.**

107

*Child's Lincoln-type rocker (Lincoln rockers
are this style but upholstered in the back and
seat), incised carving, 12½" to seat, 27½" high.
(Walnut)*

**$250.00 - 300.00.**

*Child's rocker, cane back and seat, burl veneer
incised carving, 11½" to seat, 24" high
(Walnut)*

**$165.00 - 200.00.**

*Dining table, rectangular extension, six legs, four leaves,
pendent finials, veneer panels, incised lines, 41" wide, 44"
long, 29½" high. (Walnut)*

**$550.00 - 650.00.**

*Parlor table, burl veneer on apron, incised
carving, 24" diameter, 31" high. (Walnut)*

**$375.00 - 450.00.**

*Parlor table, dark marble top, rectangular, pendent finials, incised carving, veneer panels, 30" x 22", 27½" high. (Walnut)*
$350.00 - 400.00.

*Parlor table, dark marble inserted in frame, doweled to base, rectangular, burl veneer, incised lines, 27" x 20", 29" high. (Walnut)*
$395.00 - 450.00.

*Parlor table, rectangular white marble top with rounded out corners, lacy base with tendrils, incised carving, 38" x 25", 30" high. (Walnut)*
$750.00 - 800.00.

*Parlor table, rectangular white marble top, floral incised carving, 32" x 22", 29¼" high. (Walnut)*
$375.00 - 425.00.

109

*Parlor table, rectangular, burl veneer, roundels, legs joined by central turned stretcher, 30" x 21½", 28" high. Renaisance influence. (Walnut)*
**$275.00 - 325.00.**

*Parlor table, burl veneer panels, incised lines 28" x 20", 29" high. (Walnut)*
**$225.00 - 275.00.**

*Parlor table, rectangular, incised carving, round knob finial in middle of legs, 25½" x 18½", 31" high. (Walnut)*

**$175.00 - 225.00.**

*Parlor table, rectangular, incised carving on apron and fancy base, 30" x 22", 28½" high. (Birch stained dark)* **$125.00 - 175.00**
*(Unusual store Indian wore feather headdress of suckers, Tootsie pops, and was named "Chief Watta Pop")*

Parlor table, rectangular, burl veneer, round-els, 28" x 20", 29" high. (Walnut)
**$175.00 - 225.00.**

Parlor table, burl veneer, incised carving, 32" x 22", 28½" high. (Walnut)
**$250.00 - 300.00.**

Table top parlor desk, veneer panels, made for right handed people because a retractable ink well can swing in and out from the right side as one faces the desk. Lid lifts and slants back to resemble a draft board and can be adjusted to different heights. Drawer has to be open to lift top. Trestle style. 30" x 18½", 30" tall. (Walnut)

**$475.00 - 550.00.**

Sewing stand, one drawer with drop box beneath, trestle base, burl veneer, 23½" x 16", 30" high. (Walnut)

**$375.00 - 425.00.**

## Chapter 8

# Meanwhile, Back at the Farm: Country Furniture (Circa 1845-1890)

What's a firm named "The New England Furniture Company" doing located in Grand Rapids, Michigan? It's hard to know, but it specialized in cottage furniture. Workers could enamel over softwood so that your furnishings would match your carpets, drapes, or wallpaper, or coordinate with them. You could have flowers, birds, or lines plus graining painted on surfaces. Do you like daisies? Is your favorite color blue? It's your choice. Or chamber set (bedroom suite) could be artifically grained, ornamented with dark strokes, and have a carved walnut leaf and fruit plaque attached. You could buy bright or somber sets, perhaps a table, commode, dresser, and bed all matching. If you desired a towel rack, commode, chairs, a bed, and

*Cottage bedroom set artificially grained and lined with black accent lines over pine; walnut handles. Dresser 40"x17½", 5'10" high; bed 54" wide, 73" long, 5'5" high; two cane bottom chairs with spindle backs.*

**$850.00 - 950.00 the set.**

dressing case that were not so expensive as walnut, cottage furniture would answer the purpose. Pine usually was the base wood, and the general time range was from about 1845 to 1890. Other cities produced such suites also, including formal Boston.

Many people strip sets down, letting the apple blossoms, the geraniums, or bright pastoral scenes slip down the drain in order to obtain the mellow pine beneath. Doing this destroys a form of folk art, factory produced. This may cause suites that have retained their original finish to be valuable in the future as there will be fewer of them available, and as antiquers realize, "Supply and demand determine price."

Fake graining was frequently done with the aid of brushes, combs, feathers, sponges, or similar implements. Pieces could be stained with a reddish cast and marked with dark lines to make mahogany, rosewood, or pseudo-walnut. Much was factory produced, but it could provide interesting surfaces when the technique was practiced at home. On rustic pieces, a country air resulted.

Much in the way of home furnishings prior to the 1830s was crafted at home by hand to meet a need, and native woods were utilized. In remote areas and on the frontier, the jack-of-all-trades farmer made utilitarian objects throughout most of the 1800s. Even factory furniture with simple lines may be

Child's dresser, painted blue with orange trim — a small version of a country dresser, 14" x 7", 26" high. (Pine under the paint)

**$65.00 - 90.00.**

Wood box, artificial feather graining, three simulated drawers, slant top, 37½" wide, 18½" deep, 41" high.

**$175.00 - 200.00.**

113

considered provincial, and there are many people who seek store or occupa
tional objects to create a casual comfortable decor. Some items retrieved from
offices can be on the more formal side, but since they are not, strictly speaking
home furniture, they are included here.

*Pie safe, punched tin door panels, heart designs, two drawers, back rail, 43" wide, 17" deep, 57½" high. (Walnut)*

**$100.00 - 150.00 as is;**
**$300.00 - 350.00 refinished and repaired.**

*Jelly cupboard, 42" wide, 16" deep, 64" high. (Walnut)*

**$450.00 - 525.00.**

*Trunk, dovetailed corners, wrought iron rat tail hinges, bracket feet, 43" wide, 20" deep, 23" high. (Pine)*
**$250.00 - 275.00.**

114

*Cupboard base, scalloped apron, carved walnut pulls, 45½" wide, 18½" deep, 36¼" high. (Maple and poplar)*
**$200.00 - 250.00.**

*Bucket bench, shelf above back rail, plank ends, pegs in doors, 38" wide, 16" deep, 37¼" high. (Maple and poplar)*
**$275.00 - 350.00.**

*Cradle, wings to stop draft, heart finger holds on each side, dovetailed ends, 40" long, 15" wide, 20½" high. (Walnut)*
**$200.00 - 250.00.**

*Flax wheel, 32" long, 40½" high. (Oak)*
**$325.00 - 375.00.**

*Child's desk, lift lid, back rail, trestle type legs, 18" wide, 14¼" deep, 19¼" high. (Oak)*
**$115.00 - 135.00.**

*Corner cupboard, scalloped door panels, beading beneath cornice, applied roundel, 44" wide, 33" deep, 7'3½" high. (Pine)*
**$600.00 - 700.00.**

*Commode washstand, wooden acorn handles, rounded corner stiles, 9" splash back, 29½" x 16", 30" high. (Soft maple)*
**$225.00 - 275.00.**

116

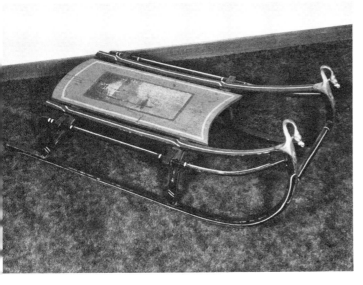

*Child's sled, original red paint with yellow design lines, pine tree painting on seat, dragon heads for rope pulls, 32" long, 14" wide, 7½" high.*
**$150.00 - 175.00.**

*Tutti Frutti store display case, pressed designs, 12½" wide, 6½" deep, 17½" high. (Oak)*
**$150.00 - 200.00.**

*Hardware store screw cabinet, 72 pie shaped drawers, excellent original condition, 22" in diameter, 33" high. (Oak)*

**$1,750.00 - 2,000.00.**

*J. & P. Coats six drawer spool cabinet, pressed designs around handles, premium original condition, 26" wide, 19½" deep, 22" high. (Cherry)*
**$350.00 - 400.00.**

*Corticelli Silk and Twist spool cabinet, round clock insert, finial designs at each front corner, ONT Our New Thread on back plates of drop pulls, shelves in cabinet behind mirror, 24" wide, 16" deep, 30" high. Museum quality. (Walnut and burled veneer)*

*Spool cabinet, white porcelain pulls, round incised designs on each drawer, 23" wide, 16" deep, 16¼" high. (Cherry)*
**$225.00 - 250.00.**

*Barber's cabinet, brass filigree panels in drop down doors, pillar stiles, applied beading, 28" wide, 14" deep, 40" high. (Walnut)*
**$550.00 - 600.00.**

*Spool cabinet, incised lines, chamfered stiles, ring pulls, 30" wide, 18½" deep, 17" high. (Cherry and birdseye maple on drawer fronts)*
**$275.00 - 350.00.**

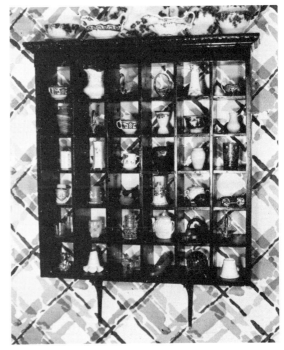

*Hotel key and mail box compartment used as mug holder, carved and incised cornice, 34" wide, 8½" deep, 37" high. (Painted over light wood)*
**$150.00 - 175.00.**

*Dental cabinet, applied roundels on drawers and decorations on stiles, molded arch on doors, pull out shelf above drawer, 30" wide, 20" deep, 5'1½" high. (Walnut)*
**$1,600.00 - 1,700.00.**

*Barber's mug cabinet, applied roundels, incised carving, brass backed ring drop pulls, 4'6" wide, 6'9" high. (Walnut)*
**$1,800.00 - 2,000.00.**

119

## Chapter 9
## Metal Magic (Circa 1850-1900s)

Have you ever driven past a yard in which an iron love seat and two side chairs painted white graced the verdant lawn as they sat under a shade tree with its spreading branches? The metal looks lacy, lovely, and elegant in a garden setting. A one-hundred-year-old foundry in Alabama is one of the establishments which is using original molds preserved from the last century to cast ornamental furniture. Urns and stands are also available, and if a vintage urn lacks ornate handles, these can be purchased individually. In addition to the price tag, the buyer pays ten percent for crating plus ten percent of the listed cost for shipping charges. Be aware that an old version is apt to be roughened by nature's sandpapery hands and may have sundry coats of people-applied paint. Some owners sandblast the surface to get rid of years of pitting before they paint their furniture a virginal white or the selected color.

*Cast iron lawn furniture — love seat and two chairs; love seat 43" wide, 36" high; chairs 15" to seat, 32" high. (Old)*

**$575.00 - 650.00 the set.**

Cast iron urn, 20" diameter, 25" high, made by 100-year-old Alabama foundry from their old molds. (Repro)

$225.00 - 250.00.

Cast iron urn, 21" diameter, 16" high, originally manufactured by the Kramer Bros. Foundry Co., Dayton, Ohio. (Old)

$450.00 - 500.00.

Cast iron green claw foot urn with cabriole knee, pineapple designs on urn, 16" diameter, 19" high. (Repro)

$125.00 - 150.00.

Cast iron urn, cherub faces on ornately designed handles, scarce, 18" diameter, 19" high, 26" handle to handle. (Old)

$275.00 - 300.00.

121

Another popular Victorian metal was brass, and beds of brass are experiencing an upsurge in interest. The late 1800s produced versions which included scrolls and other designs to achieve a dainty appearance. Families who desired to be fashionable in the days prior to 1900 cast out their ponderous wooden frames to be burned and espoused metal beds. Round posts became "the thing" at the turn of this century, and their straight lines replaced the flowing gentleness of earlier examples. Infant sizes delight the hearts of those who find them, but not a great number were made. Ornate, scroll-filled iron cribs were available and could be painted a pristine white.

The reissued "Sears, Roebuck Catalogue" for 1897 advertises adult iron beds with brass trim for $7.25 to $16.00, the latter painted with white enamel. On iron versions, the head and foot corresponded in size, but brass ones have a lower foot. Status seekers sought solid brass beds which were available in three widths, 42", 48", or 54" with their length a standard 76". Their advertised costly price was $42.50, but came with the promise that the buyer would receive "a most substantial and desirable piece of furniture which can be handed down to future generations . . ." (a faithfully fulfilled prophecy). It is interesting to contrast the cost of this one article with that of an "elegant solid oak bedroom suit" available for $16.00. This bed was six feet tall and was accompanied by a matching dresser with a mirror and a commode. Doesn't this indicate that a genuine brass bed spelled "luxury" when it was priced at almost three times as much as the three-piece wooden set? More frequently than not iron served as the base structure with brass applied around the hollow tubes and a seam line shows where the wrap met. Small decorations, spindles, and finials were constructed of solid brass, and round balls, "mushroom" knobs, or "vases" sitting atop posts were a favorite addition. These tublar beds have a heavier appearance than those with scrolls and curlicues.

A question continually asked is — how does one clean tarnished brass beds? A huffing-puffing young woman complained she'd rubbed and rubbed and used almost a whole jar of cleaner to remove the tarnish from only a small section. This effort had taken her days and days! (a quote). Would anything hasten the process and reduce the work? A professional product is oxalic acid but since it is a poison, selective housewives do not desire to stock it. Often the reason for the tough rub job may be attributed to a lacquer coating applied to protect the surface from darkening from hand and air contact. So — buy a good paint remover and let it work for you because, after the lacquer is taken off, the surface can be polished with ease to gleam. If lacquer is reapplied to the clean surface, work rapidly as it dries almost instantaneously and it is wise to work in a well ventilated room. A mask over the nose and mouth helps protect one from inhaling fumes when paint removing or using a lacquer spray. Paint stores carry such supplies. The huff-puff frustrated housewife called back elated because this method readily helped her achieve her goal — a glowing, grime-free bed.

Thrifty housewives might sprinkle salt on inside-out rinds of lemons or grapefruits, and this grit 'n acid combination rubs off tarnish. Any residue can be washed and rinsed off.

Small pieces of brass and copper can be soaked very briefly in vinegar. Rub with fine steel wool, rinse in clean water, and dry. This acetic acid solution can give golden brass an orange copper color if exposed more than a minute or so, and it is necessary to watch carefully in order to avoid this transformation. Brass is an alloy of copper and zinc.) Large articles can be wrapped with newspaper wet with vinegar.

Brass hall trees — upright tubular posts with hooks at the top for holding hats and coats and supported by tripod legs — are desirable. Vintage ones sell for $125.00 and up, and current revivals, available through import shops, can be purchased. Glowing metal with no indications of a softening shading with age, no signs of use, and workmanship which usually doesn't compare with that in older examples, are indicative of newer types. Metal, both iron and brass, was a definite part of Victorian era furniture, and, if you don't want a repro (reproduction), examine your item well before you forfeit your money.

# Chapter 10
# Wispy Wicker (Circa 1850-1920)

"Creak, groan," the generous-size, wide wicker chair mutters when its occupant settles, moves, or rises; and, minutes after the sitter departs, the chair continues to protest as it readjusts its fibers. It looks delicate but is sturdy and appears cool enough to serve as furniture on a porch of the past or a present day patio.

*Wicker chair, ornately designed, originally, pressed cane seat, circa 1885, 24" wide, 16" to seat, 40" high. (Flat rattan over birch)*
**$300.00 - 350.00.**

Wicker is a generic term for furniture made from fibers such as rattan, reed, willow, and paper twisted spirals. Its popularity ascends and descends, and wicker furniture has been in, out, and now is in favor once again. So if grandma and grandpa stashed theirs in the loft or attic, it's in style to dig it out and revitalize it. Perhaps colorful new covers will freshen the early century cretonne slip-out cushions, or bits of raveling rattan may require repair, or a sagging cane seat may need replacing. Perhaps the stained brown, green, or natural tones (with a clear varnish finish) are displeasing and a paint job seems indicated. White is frequently chosen and yields an airy appearance almost as ethereal as Shakespeare's mischievous fairy Puck in "A Midsummer Night's Dream."

Generally, wicker furniture was made in the late 1800s, continuing in production through the 1920s, and was hauled off to the attic, garbage dump, junk yard, or pyre as the 1940s commenced. Now capricious Miss Popularity is provocatively smiling on it again, and it can be purchased used or recently manufactured. Much has an Oriental parentage, although various factories in the United States produced wicker creations also.

Generally speaking, the old wicker of the mid-1800s was quite plain, and graduated at the turn of this century to ornate styles with fibers tortuously twisted in floral designs with curls and balls in abundance. Designs returned to plain in the early decades of the 1900s. Many seekers prefer the more decorative types and request objects with ornamental curlicues and non-essential loops.

*Wicker sofa, painted white, 65" wide, 17" to seat, 37" high.*
**$250.00 - 275.00.**

*Wicker plant stand, 14¼" diameter, 36" high.*
**$90.00 - 110.00.**

*Wicker baby buggy, parasol can bend down or stay up, metal wheels with wooden spokes, 52" long, 16½" wide, 56½" high.*
**$600.00 - 675.00.**

Examine the ornate buggy pictured. A few years previously, when the current owners' son was almost brand new, the young couple used to stroll the streets of their small town pushing him in his unique carriage. People stopped the trio to comment and ladies gushed over the adorable sight. The baby, sensing admiration and loving it, smiled with delight, never realizing that his vehicle was as much an object of attention as its adorable wee occupant. The carriage's parasol, still intact, folds away or unfolds its silk screen to shade baby. In prime condition it is valued at $675.00 - $750.00. A tattered, battered frame with missing loops, the umbrella long gone, might have a $75.00 tag with an invitation to "make an offer" included. Child sizes for dolls are sought by collectors who want their cherubs displayed in normal settings. Pricewise their value varies greatly depending on factors previously discussed. One in diminutive doll size, of similar style, and in pristine condition as is the baby buggy depicted might list at $250.00.

Pieces made in wicker include fern stands, tables (round and rectangular), a variety of chairs, sofas, book or display cases, bird cages; and, following the Victorian period, in the 1920s, lamps appeared.

Wicker with its casual carefree appearance is groaning its way back into homes as furnishings for family rooms and recreation areas, and is comfortable indoors or out.

# Chapter 11

## At Era's End: Golden Oak, Mission, and Stickley (Circa 1890-1920)

Exit walnut, circa 1880. Why? For one thing, the virgin American forests had been stripped of most of the trees of this species. Walnut wood became scarce. Another reason — Dame Fashion coyly awarded her smiles to metal beds and nodded to oak. Those who wanted to be in style scrambled to follow the new trends which began as the Victorian era was coming to a close and continued into the early decades of the 1900s.

Most sources place Golden Oak in the 1900s, after Mission Oak's impact was felt. However, based on research at the Grand Rapids, Michigan, public library, Golden Oak precedes Mission by a few years. It entered the scene at least by 1890 because the Manestee Manufacturing Company, a firm located

*Combination sideboard, china closet, beveled mirror, convex glass, incised carving, applied decorations, 44" wide, 19" deep, 5'11½" high. (Oak)*

in the Michigan city by that name, advertised a queen-size golden oak sideboard over six feet high with a 23″ by 48″ top (that's almost two feet by four feet) in that year. It had carved feet, two swell front drawers, and doors with carved panels. A buyer could secure all that massiveness for fourteen dollars.

Three years later the Widdicomb Furniture Company, Grand Rapids, advertised bedroom and dining room furniture in oak, curly birch, birdseye maple, and mahogany. By 1895, a buyer could purchase golden birch, oak (both white and golden), and mahogany from this company. The ad evolved to birdseye maple, quartered oak, and mahogany veneers in 1899.

But, take note of this. White ash, a more placid wood than oak which it resembles, was made into suits from 1850 through at least 1876. It was slightly less expensive than its counterparts in walnut. A three piece chamber suit (not suite) embracing bureau, washstand, and bedstead, with wooden tops sold for $23.75-46.75. In walnut, it cost $27.50-51.00. Since ash and oak are similar in appearance, many people inspect ash and call it oak. Elm also is an oak look alike and was available as a furniture wood in the 1880s.

Golden Oak was not hand carved. Instead, a design pressed into the back of chairs with a metal die proved decorative and currently young people search for sets of these chairs which are called pressed backs. Many have pressed cane seats. (The cane comes in pre-woven sheets, is cut to size, soaked, and stretched over the hole. The ends are pushed into a glue-filled groove with a spleen covering driven in to hold the seat taut.)

*Pressed back chair, three front turned rungs, pressed cane seat, 17½″ to seat, 40½″ high. (Oak)*
**Set of four: $100.00 - 120.00 each.**

*China buffet, convex glass, fret work design on lower glass door, claw feet, back rail with beveled mirror, 41″ wide, 16″ deep, 50″ high. (Oak)*
**$725.00 - 800.00.**

128

Round oak pedestal tables have extra leaves and expand to seat many people. If the pedestal has claw feet, it carries a heftier price tag. Sideboards and china cabinets (especially those with convex glass) are popular. The washstands and dressers are sought.

*Commode washstand, incised lines, floral inset cuts on doors, drawer and back rail, 31" x 15", 30" high. (Oak)*
**$250.00 - 300.00.**

*China cabinet, two doors, straight glass, 42" wide, 19" deep, 57½" high. (Oak)*
**$425.00 - 475.00.**

*Combination bookcase and writing desk, applied decorations, fancy fret work by mirror, brass handles, 39½" wide, 12" deep, 71" high. (Oak)*
**$525.00 - 600.00.**

*Combination bookcase and writing desk, simple incised decorations, convex glass, 32" wide, 10½" deep, 70" high. (Oak)*
**$425.00 - 475.00.**

*Pressed back chair, three front turned rungs, pressed cane seat, 18" to seat, 38½" high. (Oak)*
**Set of four: $100.00 - 120.00 each.**

*Pressed back arm chair, three front turned rungs, square cane seat, roller coaster arms, 24½" wide, 17½" to seat, 39" high. (Oak)*
**$155.00 - 175.00.**

*Pressed back child's rocker, rolled arms, five spindled back, 11" to seat, 27" high, (Oak)*
**$135.00 - 155.00.**

*Rocking chair, pressed back, rolled arms, flat spindled back, leather seat, 16" to seat, 38½" high. (Oak)*

**$225.00 - 250.00.**

*Cane chair, five spindle splayed back, U-shape seat, brass tips on finials, 17½" to seat, 41" high. (Maple)*
**$85.00 - 100.00.**

*Rocking chair, child's, splat back, inset seat, 12" to seat, 26½" high. (Oak)*
**$110.00 - 135.00.**

*Rocking chair, continuous bent back, caned back and U-shaped seat, 14" to seat, 30" high. (Mixed light woods)*
**$125.00 - 145.00.**

*Shaving stand, oval mirror, serpentine drawer and doors, applied claw feet on front legs, 17" x 11", 46" high. (Oak)*
**$475.00 - 525.00.**

131

*Hat rack, inset mirror, brass tendrils around mirror, 23¼ x 15". (Oak and brass)*

**$125.00 - 135.00.**

*Combination ice box and buffet, pressed designs on two doors, beveled mirror, scalloped apron, ice box on right, shelves for food on left, 46" wide, 22" deep, 69½" high. (Oak) Museum quality.*

*Umbrella stand, metal pan at base, clover hand hold in top, 11½" wide, 10½" deep, 35½" high. (Oak)*
**$75.00 - 95.00.**

132

As has been stated, birdseye maple, possibly with a Louis XV flair, was mentioned in a Grand Rapids ad in 1893. The "eyes" apparently are buds which do not break through to the outer surface and make a bird's eye size figure on veneer sliced from maple trees. This figure is found more often in maple than in other types of trees.

*Dresser, large swinging mirror, scalloped top, cabriole legs, 46" wide, 22" deep, 72" high. (Birdseye maple and maple)*
**$225.00 - 275.00.**

*Chiffonier, swinging mirror, cabriole legs, 30" wide, 21½" deep, 66½" high. (Birdseye maple and maple)*
**$225.00 - 245.00.**

*Love seat, arm chair, and rocking chair, tufted backs, upholstered seats. (Maple stained mahogany with red aniline dye)*
**$850.00 - 1,000.00 the set.**

Also around the turn of the century it was popular to stain maple red to emulate mahogany, and the suits which resulted were sturdy enough to compare with Mission Oak. Refinishers regret that such aniline dye does not want to come out but adheres stubbornly to the wood.

Straight stocky lines — that's Mission Oak. A row of straight solid lumber separated by air space — that's the look of a Mission Oak sofa — functional, sturdy, utilitarian, substantial. Color it dark brown and put black leather cushions on it. There's a piece of furniture that'll last, but the style didn't. It was current from about 1895-1910 and many desks, clocks, chairs, and tables were made in this forceful manner. It is a product of the English Arts and Craft Movement when designers wanted to forget lavish styles and return to plain usefulness. Mission was developed in America so it's a native.

Gustav Stickley of Binghamton, New York, promoted the sale of bungalow homes which were inexpensive and casual. Stickley designed and manufactured "Craftsman" furniture to go inside these houses, but someone dubbed the homes "Spanish Mission" style, and the name leached itself onto the furniture as well.

Most people associate this look with the missions the Spanish opened to convert Indians during exploration days in the old Southwest, but it was really a promotional gimmick title to sell abodes and furnishings.

*Arm chair, leather seat and back, claw feet, 19" to seat, 38" high. (Maple)*

**$150.00 - 200.00.**

*Rocking chair, Mission style, 17" to seat, 34" high. (Oak)*

**$75.00 - 100.00.**

This style is coming back into prominence, and "Stickley" is being bandied about as "the name" in Mission Oak.

One of the men who influenced Mission Oak's design was William Morris, a leader of the English Arts and Crafts Movement. He promoted handcraftsmanship and wanted furniture to be functional. An early lounging chair with an adjustable rod which could be moved so that the back could be upright or slanted was named the Morris chair. Its lines resembled Mission, but the chair itself pre-dates Mission. The pictured example is a patented adaptation with a push button which adjusts the back automatically and is a later version of his chair.

Arm chair, later Morris type, push button on right arm moves back up and down, 17" to seat, 36" high. (Oak)
**$125.00 - 150.00.**

Metal plaque found on Morris type chair.

# Chapter 12
# Bits and Pieces

This chapter is like sweeping fragments under the rug. Since Victorians copied everything, but everything, this gathers up the left over bits and pieces.

## Oriental

The Oriental feel was a late Victorian deviation (after 1875). Bamboo, either faked with lines on maple or genuine, formed tables and chairs. An elaborate imported settee dated Paris, 1888, has rich panels of silver and mother of pearl. A full length carved dragon crawls across its pierced back. The dragonhead arm supports face the world fiercely and fearlessly. That's chinoiserie (a Chinese appeal).

*Chinoiserie sofa, Oriental influence, mother of pearl and silver inlay on round panels, two dragonhead arms, full dragon as crest, pierced carved back, 4' 1" outside measurement 17½" to seat, 43" high.*

**$1,650.00 - 1,750.00.**

*Parlor table, bamboo turnings for legs, edging, and shelf supports, 18½" x 18½", 29" high. (Oak)*

**$90.00 - 125.00.**

## Bentwood

In about 1840, Michael Thonet of Vienna, Austria, began to mass produce
chairs bent to be structurally strong yet pleasing to the eye. Thousands of
chairs, including rockers, were mass produced and are still being made. Light
weight side chairs were utilized in club rooms.

## Windsor

There is a romantic tale that roly-poly King George III of England (ruled
1760-1820) sought shelter in a rube's cottage during a storm. His chair fit the
monarch's corpulent torso so well that the king ordered a set for Windsor
Castle from whence they supposedly derived their name. "False," roar histo-
rians. "Those chairs pre-date George by at least fifty years and are probably
named for the town, not the castle."

At any rate, the chairs emigrated to the English colonies in America and
were made in Philadelphia circa 1725, years before George ascended the
throne. They've been made ever since, including the addition of rockers by
United States craftsmen.

*Windsor rocking chair, rolled arms, rod back, U-*
*shaped cane seat, 17" to seat, 33½" high. (Oak)*
**$145.00 - 175.00.**

*Child's Bentwood high chair, with tray and foot rest,*
*38" high. (Maple stained mahogany)*
**$160.00 - 195.00.**

The familiar captain's chair, firehouse chair, or bar stool is a debased Windsor. A good Windsor has a back with many contoured spindles (seven to nine). A thick plank shield-shaped or elliptical seat was made of one piece of wood cut out in a saddle shape to fit the human body. The front edge would be chamfered (cut in at a slant). Windsors were made of various woods and generally were painted. The ends of the bent back and legs usually went clear through the seat. Later copies do not have these desirable characteristics, but when you see "sticks" in the back of a chair, think "Windsor."

*Windsor type chair, plank seat, splayed legs, 17½" to seat, 30½" high. (Basswood seat, hickory turning, oak and maple legs, turned rung, and spindles)*
**$65.00 - 85.00.**

*Rocking chair, child's, spindle back, round plank seat 10½" to seat, 26½" high. (Oak, maple, hickory)*
**$125.00 - 155.00.**

## Shakers

This separatist religious sect called itself the United Society of Believers but to those who observed the way they danced to worship God, another title seemed more descriptive. The celibate brothers and sisters never danced together. That was forbidden. It was strictly individual — men lined up on one side, women alone on the other, their feet shuffling along, their bodies quaking as their extended arms quivered. Spectators dubbed them Shakers because of these tremulous movements.

Devotedly they considered work worship, and all their labors were completed in the best manner possible to honor God. The nucleus of the group came from England in 1774 under the leadership of Sister Ann Lee (originally Lees). Perhaps because her own married life did not prove rewarding, she advocated a single status for believers, and the only children were those the Shakers adopted or the offsprings of couples married before they joined.

They were an inventive people and developed labor-saving devices which included farm implements and machinery, washing machines, cheese presses, and a form of condensed milk. The Society was strong and powerful at one time and packaged improved garden seeds, made better brooms, and crafted chairs (mainly rockers) for sale. The lack of procreation helped deplete its ranks and the strict rules plus plain living did not attract many converts.

Shaker furniture was functional and plain of line, as austere as were the lives of the members, and this very strict purity of both purpose and design is one of the secrets of its integrity and beauty. Colonies flourished in various states including Kentucky, Ohio, Massachusetts, New York, Maine, and Connecticut. Brothers skilled with wood working tools selected native woods including pine, fruitwoods, walnut, and maple to use in crafting desks, chests, tables, beds, stands, footstools, clothes racks, or whatever was required. After the brothers made chair frames, it was the duty of assigned sisters to complete the seats. When chairs have a series of parallel slats to form the back supports, they are referred to as ladder backs, and many Shaker versions were fashioned in this way.

*Shaker type chair, splint seat, ladder back (a true Shaker would have no turned legs or rungs and straight slats), 14" to seat. (Maple)*
**$60.00 - 70.00.**

Various colors of interwoven fabric tape formed attractive seats, and sometimes the back did not have slats but was patterned in a like manner. Splint, flat thin strips of oak or hickory, could slant across in triangular fashion or present a block formation. Marsh-grown flag provided material for rush seats with their four equal-sized adjoining triangles. The slender tough long stems of a climbing palm (rattan) provided cane which usually was woven in a diamond design. Synthetic cane, spiral strands of paper, and paper splint frequently replace the natural seat materials of yore.

The Shakers began selling chairs as the 1700s came to a close and by the 1850s the chairs had standard numbers on them. The Shakers also acquired a gold transfer trademark which included the society name. Perhaps because work and worship were as one to them, their products represent quality. There are critics who consider their efforts the epitome of country furniture, and many emulate their work.

## Patented Furniture

Patents were issued for various types of furniture in the late 1800s. Rockers placed on springs or on platforms so that they did not cut the carpet with sharp runners, or creep across the room as one gently tilted backward and forward, were comfortable. There were various types of folding chairs and tables as well.

One oak item was for children only. It was a high chair which could be converted into a stroller to meet the two needs. A more elaborate kind could be turned into a cradle bed besides.

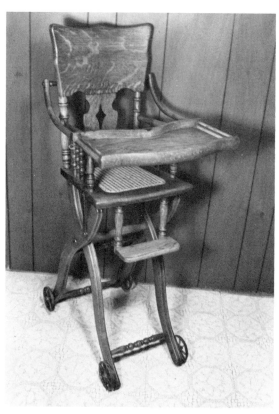 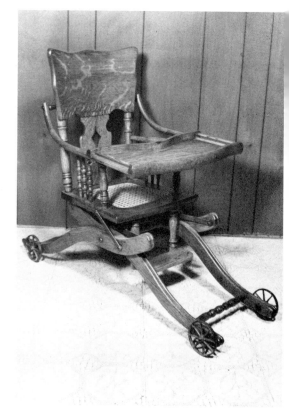

Child's high chair in upright position, pressed cane seat, metal wheels, pierced back splat, 17" wide at tray, 41" high. (Oak)

Child's high chair in stroller position, 31" long, 28½" high.

$250.00 - 275.00.

*Platform rocker, padded arms, pillow rest, 14½" to seat, 40" high. (Walnut)*
**$165.00 - 200.00.**

*Reclining chair, upholstered, fold up foot rest, 17" to seat, 44" high. (Walnut)*
**$200.00 - 275.00.**

*Platform rocker, incised lines, turned posts, 14½" to seat, 42½" high. (Maple)*
**$155.00 - 175.00.**

*Platform rocker, pillow rest, brass tips on finials, patented May 23, 1878, 16" to seat, 42" high. (Oak)*
**$165.00 - 195.00.**

141

Patented heavy adult beds folded to form chests, desks, wardrobes, book cases, mantels, or combinations thereof. When the frame was prone for sleeping, it resembled most bedsteads. When it was folded into its compartment, it took on the appearance of a case piece and served a different purpose. It had a split personality. Since these were available in the early decades of the 1900s, movie goers laughed at scenes in which "Murphy beds" folded at crucial moments, at times giving an occupant an unscheduled ride to an inside view.

*Folding fireside arm chair, 15½" to seat, 39" high. (Walnut)*

**$135.00 - 165.00.**

*Child's folding side chair, cane seat, 12¼ to seat, 24 high. (Maple and oak)*

**$75.00 - 90.00.**

## Let There Be Music

In the late 1800s, a Swedish immigrant became part owner of a company which manufactured organs. When small towns around were organizing churches or establishing a music fund, he would visit them and donate an organ to the congregation. In those days there were wealthy farmers who would decide their families must have musical instruments. Naturally they placed their orders with the generous religious gentleman whose benevolence provided him with a neat profit.

Producing music was a difficult task, a session which tested one's coordination and provided exercise. The player pumped vigorously with her feet, sometimes having a knee action as well, and her fingers busily manipulated stops as her hands pounded on the keyboard. Some church organs were constructed so that a young boy could pump the bellows from a crouched, secluded position behind the organ so that playing did not provide such an exhausting work-out. If the lad dozed during the long sermon, no hymn of departure was included in the service. If the bellows were bad — wheeze.

In contrast, music boxes were easy to play because a flick of a switch provided a flow of song. Switzerland's ingenuity produced music boxes around 1825. The early versions had a cylinder (a pin plucked the barrel to produce the tune) and a sounding barrel in a wooden case. They tinkled out various itemized tunes. Later versions afforded greater variety because these had disc tune sheets which were removable and could be changed as desired. Cases could be plain or ornate with inlay.

*Organ, #248 Packard, Fort Wayne, Indiana, three sections with mirror in top part, ornately decorated, 44½" wide, 23" deep, 6' 7" high. (Walnut)*
**$750.00 - 900.00.**

*Organ, Cornish Co., Washington, New Jersey, one section, 42" wide, 22½" deep, 43" high.*
**$500.00 - 550.00.**

*Organ stool, fringed top, metal base, 14½" x 14¼", 20" to 23" high as it raises and lowers.*
**$75.00 - 95.00.**

*Organ lamp, brass, adjusts from 5'2" to 6'11" in height, patented June 18, 1878.*
**$950.00 - 1,100.00.**

# Kerosene Lamps

Circa 1860, when Canadian doctor-geologist Abraham Gesner developed an improved lighting oil refined from coal (coal oil), it proved to be a real asset. Whale oil was smoky and smelly, and some fuels were dangerously explosive. Kerosene was cleaner and safer. By the late 1800s fancy parlor lamps, both hanging and table models, developed. A patent date may be present on metal portions which lets one know that his lamp was made sometime after the last date mentioned.

*Pressed glass kerosene lamp, 21" high.*
**$55.00 - 65.00.**

*Hanging lamp, prisms, handpainted shade, brass shade support and appendages; handpainted font.*
**$450.00 - 500.00.**

144

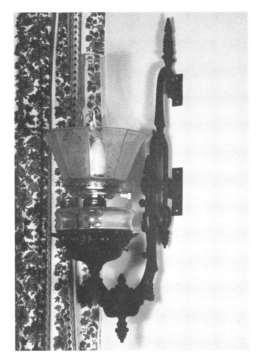

*Bracket lamp, iron supports, etched shade.*
**$80.00 - 95.00.**

*Table lamp, green slag shade with fringe and brass dividers, embossed font, brass stand, height adjusts from 5'2" to over 6'.*
**$750.00 - 850.00.**

*Hanging lamp, prisms, handpainted shade, brass shade support and appendages, handpainted font.*
**$400.00 - 450.00.**

## Frames

Frames in all shapes and sizes appeared during the Victorian era. Circa 1850 deep oval examples can be seen on the walls in some of the pictures throughout this book (including the preceding page under lamps). Crisscross ends were popular and had carved leaves at the corners. At times porcelain "buttons" provided ornamentation instead.

Some rectangular versions are frames within frames, and if a portion is damaged, it is possible to take them apart to preserve the good section intact.

Gold leaf decorated many, and it is genuine when it is applied in 3½" widths, as noted by hairline cracks. A 5½" span denotes an imitation type. Fashion prints, pictures of ancestors, pictures formed from human hair, dried floral arrangements, and documents were framed. There seemed to be a reverence for the dear departed which resulted in religious pictures and morbid memorials dedicated to the deceased.

*Multi-linear frame alternating with gilt, 26" x 30". (Oak)*
**$35.00 - 50.00.**

*Crisscross frame with leaf corners fashion print is hand colored, 16" x 17½" (Walnut)*

**$35.00 - 45.00.**

*Multi-linear gold frame, red felt liner, 30" x 35".*

**$50.00 - 65.00.**

Little girls of four or five had to sit still and laboriously practice sewing stitches. When they were qualified, they displayed their ability as they practiced by making "samplers" with their A,B,Cs, some depicting Bible verses, proverbs, flowers, birds, and animals. They were usually signed by the maker and dated. Older versions are taller than they are wide. As the 1800s progressed, the rectangle became wider than it was long. Interesting wall groupings can be formed with passé frames.

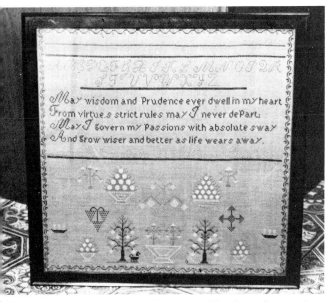

Framed sampler, Ann R. Thompson, Windsor, Connecticut, 1834; ABCs plus saying, trees, and designs, 19¼" x 19".

**$225.00 - 275.00.**

Frame with 1888 wedding certificate, 18" x 21". (Walnut with gold insert)

**$55.00 - 65.00.**

Rococo-type frame with mirror inserted, gold, 24½" x 28½"

**$65.00 - 85.00.**

Prang chromolithograph, First Lesson in Music, 19" x 22"

**$150.00 - 175.00.**

147

## Wall Pockets

Wall pockets were both utilitarian and decorative, and 'most anything could be tucked away inside of them. What better place could be found to keep slippers handy in a bed chamber or to keep the weekly newspaper near pa's chair? A double picture frame type was advertised in the 1897 Sears Roebuck Catalogue, a later version than those shown here.

*Wall pocket, leaf corners on crisscross frame, leaf tendrils form top, picture of cross with flowers, 14" wide, 26" high. (Walnut, imitation leather sides)*
**$75.00 - 100.00.**

*Wall pocket with chain to hold drop front, hinged at base, 17" wide, 25" high. (Walnut)*
**$75.00 - 100.00.**

*Wall pocket, incised carving, leaves, chain holds drop front, hinged at base, 11½" wide, 24" high. (Walnut)*

**$75.00 - 100.00.**

## Spice Boxes

Spices — like sugar — came in lumps and hunks, or in seed form, not neatly ground in handy containers ready for consumption as they do today. Small drawers in a wooden enclosure held cinnamon sticks or the nutmeg to be grated. Most were made in a light wood stained dark but an occasional walnut one is found.

*Spice box, eight drawers, porcelain knobs, 10" wide, 18" high. (Pine)*

**$85.00 - 100.00.**

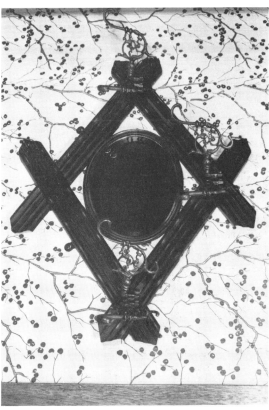

*Metal hat rack, beveled oval mirror, diamond-shaped frame, three sets of double hooks, 25" wide, 20" high.*

**$80.00 - 100.00.**

## Toilet Articles

The word "toilet" had a different connotation in Victorian days than it does today. The term formerly applied to grooming. The meaning covered the entire process of getting presentable, from climbing into the old wash tub to bathe, putting on one's clothes, to combing one's hair. Associated articles were called toilet articles, and a mirror could be termed a toilet. Looking glasses were also referred to as plates, perhaps a shortened form of the phrase a "plate of glass" (a thin sheet of coated glass). Mirrors combined with hat hooks hung in the main hall and afforded one a quick inspection for escaping wisps of hair when one made his entrance or departed.

Various types of comb cases hung on the wall near the wash bowl and pitcher which were necessary prior to the days when bathrooms were incorporated into homes. Some comb cases included toilets (mirrors), towel bars, and holders for the matches needed to light the lamps or candles when required.

One side held fresh matches, the other, burned-outs. Comb case designs followed furniture patterns of the period. Since combs and brushes were called "toilet sets," maybe these wall accessories should be termed "toilet cases."

Comb case, incised lines, cut out design in back, 12" wide, 12" high. (Walnut)

$95.00 - 135.00.

Shaving mirror and comb case box with lid, incised carving, leaf crest, 12" wide, 24" high. (Walnut)

$100.00 - 150.00.

Shaving mirror and comb case, incised carving, leaf carved crest, 15" wide, 26" high. (Walnut)

$100.00 - 150.00.

Combination towel bar comb case with match holders, incised carving, 12" wide, 26" high. (Walnut)

$150.00 - 175.00.

## Wall Shelves

Since Victorians liked doodads, wall shelves appeared in abundance. If you want to go Continental, say the housewives of the 1800s enjoyed bijouterie. It merely is another way of saying they found pleasure in trinkets of all sorts.

*Wall shelf, leaf tendril design with bird crest, 10"*
*wide, 3" deep, 15½" high. (Walnut)*
**$75.00 - 100.00.**

*Wall shelf, three graduated shelves, cut out designs,*
*16" wide, 28" high. (Light wood stained dark)*
**$65.00 - 80.00.**

## Do You Have the Time?

Addle-pated, that's how villagers in Connecticut might have referred to Eli Terry. In his day, clocks were built to order, piece by piece, but Eli felt there ought to be a better way. He signed a contract to produce four thousand clock movements in three years, and his New England neighbors remarked, "It can't be done." In order to beat his deadline, Terry designed new machinery. He did not use expensive hand-fashioned brass but included cheaper wooden works instead, and he and his workmen made identical parts which were interchangeable. This made it possible for Eli Terry to mass produce his product. He fulfilled his contract, and, in doing so helped start the modern factory system. He also made it possible for ordinary homes to have clocks since the cost of making them was reduced. Later, machine stamped brass works were made inexpensively. In 1831, Terrysville, Connecticut, was named in his honor.

One of his workers, Seth Thomas, became well known in the clock industry. He worked at Plymouth Hollow until 1866 when the community's name was changed to "Thomaston," Connecticut, for him. Such name changes are noted on the papers which are pasted on the back insides of clock cases and help to date clocks, although their real purpose was to keep dust out. Rectangular ogee clocks (cases with a double S type curve molding) were stylish from about 1848-1888, and the term mantle clock refers to any kind that sits upon a shelf. Wall clocks hang up, but some are designed to both sit and hang.

Frequently a clock repair man penciled the date that he made repairs on the back of the case. This provides some information about the clock.

*Mantle clock, brass frame on porcelain face, mirror side with finials, made by F. Kroeber, 14" wide, 14" high. (Walnut)*
$250.00 - 300.00.
*Clock shelf, applied shell design, 27" wide, 7" deep, 9½" high.*
$125.00 - 150.00.

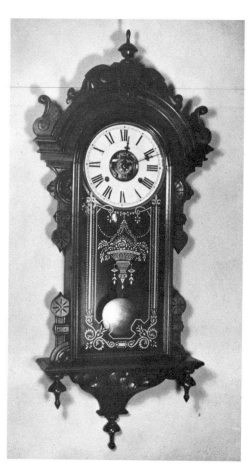

*Regulator clock, Columbia head, patented March 21, 1876, Gilbert Clock Co., 15" wide, 33" high. (Walnut)*
$625.00 - 700.00.

*Mantle clock, applied decorations, porcelain face, 16" wide, 23" high. (Oak)*
$225.00 - 250.00.

# The Tester Bed

"General Ulysses S. Grant slept here," the previous owner boasted when he sold this bed to its current owners. Presumably it once occupied a chamber in Magnolia Hall, an estate in Cario, Illinois, and the General stayed there during one of his Civil War campaigns. A canopy or tester top formerly was supported by the tall posts. This bed is from early in the period.

*Gentleman's chair, tufted back, eclectic features, 14½" to seat, 36½" high; part of a five piece set including one side chair, two large arm chairs, one small arm chair, and one sofa. (Walnut)*
**$6,000.00 for the set.**

*Four poster bedstead, three arch panels and scalloped sides on headboard, double casters on legs, 58" wide, 79" long, 8'7" high; the 2'6" to top of the mattress meant that originally a bed step was needed to get into the bed. (Walnut and rosewood)*
**$2,500.00 - 3,250.00.**

## It's Eclectic

As has been reiterated, it's difficult to classify Victorian furniture because machines made it easy for workmen to copy what they liked from previous periods. The gentleman's chair in the photograph vividly reflects this eclectic tendency. Note that the legs are a Louis IV type. The front apron gently curves and the back is an oval, both Louis XV characteristics. The Egyptian heads serving as arm supports and the profile featured in the back medallion are Empire overtones. The cresting and roundels represent a Renaissance adaptation. This was not a chair for the average household but knew aristocratic surroundings in the late 1800s when the wealthy wanted lavish furniture.

153

# Second Empire

Empire provided an entrance into Victorian styles before losing its popular appeal. At the turn of the twentieth century — behold — Empire returned with a 1900-1920ish feel. Thus, facetiously, one could say that Victorian furniture is the filling between slices of Empire. This would not be exactly true as not much of the new Empire was made, and Golden Oak and Mission were the dominant 1890s-1915 styles; but it provides a different closing touch. The first was hand crafted while the second Empire was machined. Chapter 13, pages 73-74, provides quick tips on how to note the difference between the hand crafted Empire, pre 1840, and circa 1900 machine made furniture.

*Library table, oval, scrolled supports attached to rolled legs, 48" x 29½", 29½" high. An early twentieth century reproduction of empire.*
**$110.00 - 125.00.**

## Chapter 13
## Signs of the Times

"Container Buyers," "Thinking of Your Own Container?" Ad headings such as these appear in trade journals geared for dealers. They encourage the purchase of twenty foot cases filled with selected Scottish or English "antiques" for resale to a United States market, and some shops specialize in such European imports.

At times it is possible to spot English furniture immediately. For example, drawer pulls tend to be distinctive with bails and drops which have a heavier, more solid appearance than native counterparts. When drawers are dovetailed, there are usually four or five tiny rather than three or four large dovetails. Vintage English dressers frequently have dust liners and a mid support often was placed on drawer bottoms. Indigenous older pieces generally do not share these characteristics.

Chairs tend to have a solid, stocky appearance. Wardrobes, necessary in yester-year homes which lacked closets, may be huge with decorative veneer-

*English wardrobe (armoire), oval molding, bun feet, brass bail pulls on base drawer, cornice, mirror framed by molding, 50″ wide, 21″ deep, 7′ high. (Birch)*
**$375.00 - 425.00.**

ing and mirrors, and frequently matched the bed and dressing table to form a suit. American styles can have plainer lines, may be of solid walnut, and may not be so huge as these "loners" which are not part of a set.

Many washstands display colorful tile splash backs. Spiral turnings which resemble twisted rope occur. If a beginner familiarizes himself or herself with the contents of antique shops where furniture which was made in the United States is shown, his or her eyes become accustomed to appearance and construction differences. Most dealers will tell neophytes which wares are native and which are foreign, but be aware that the British Isles are supplying shops with merchandise.

Common imports include oak drop leaf tables which are very slender when their deep leaves are down but become spacious surfaces when these are raised. Oak draw tables (sometimes termed refectory tables) have terminal leaves which can be pulled out level with the top surface when needed or folded back or pushed down and under the main section when not in use. They must have a sturdy base in order to retain their balance. A scrub top table folds in squarish lines and when opened shows a work surface which is not finished. The housewife undoubtedly kneaded dough or rolled pastries on it and could scrub it after her duties were done for the day.

Examine the pictures to note obvious differences so that you can be knowledgeable and exclaim, "That's an import!" when next you see an English piece.

*English balloon back chair, slip seat held with dowel, serpentine apron, 38" high. (Beech)*
**$95.00 - 125.00.**

156

*English washstand (termed wash hand stand) with alternating brown solid color and designed green and blue tile splash back. Marble top is gray, white, brown mottled. Pad foot. 36" wide, 18" deep, 43½" high. (Walnut)*

**$300.00 - 350.00.**

*English balloon back chair, slip seat held with dowel, straight apron, 38″ high. (Beech)*
**$95.00 - 125.00.**

*English dressing table, swing mirror with decks, brass bail handles, incised carving, 41½″ wide, 20″ deep, 61″ high. (Birch)*
**$325.00 - 375.00.**

*Chippendale-type side chair, ball and claw foot, lyre back splat, unusual arm treatment, mahogany veneer, 40″ high. (Birch stained dark combined with mahogany veneer)*
**$275.00 - 325.00.**

*English washstand (termed wash hand stand), splash back has framed, glass covered fabric, marble top, cast bail handle on fake drawer, 30″ wide, 18″ deep, 52″ high. (Light wood stained dark)*
**$175.00 - 225.00.**

English child's dresser, metal pendent pulls, swinging bevelled mirror with decks, possible base alteration, 29" wide, 18½" deep, 53½" high. (Walnut)
**$125.00 - 175.00.**

English sideboard, applied leaf molding on two doors, carved leaves on stiles, leaf carved pediment, old red paint inside, 42" wide, 18" deep, 5'10" high. (Mahogany)

**$550.00 - 650.00.**

English hall table, applied decoration on front apron resembles coat of arms, pointed gallery, 41½" wide, 16" deep, 33" high. (Walnut)
**$225.00 - 275.00.**

*Common washstand, crafted reproduction marked as such with name 'Witter," acorn pull not typical of oak pieces which usually had metal; top 23" x 18", 34½" high. (Oak)*

**$200.00 - 250.00.**

*Pressed back chair, reproduction sold as such, turned spindles, legs, and rungs, plank seat made from many equal sized pieces of wood, 18" to seat, 41½" high. (Oak)*

**$60.00 - 75.00.**

Reproductions are rampant. It is disturbing to realize that some firms surreptitiously are selling new skillfully executed furniture replicas as old. No harm occurs if a person buys a copy and knows it is a reproduction, but when one is led to believe the purchase is a vintage piece, the dealing is questionable. Here's a quick lesson on how to detect age differences.

A dealer stated, "If someone asks me for a rapid appraisal, I ask them to bring me a drawer, and I can give them quite a bit of information." Another antiquer affirms that drawers are a good clue to furniture age.

1. Examine a drawer. It may or may not have dovetail joints (a "v" shape which interlocks into another piece in jigsaw puzzle fashion). If it does, handmade ones will have scribe lines to show how deeply the maker should cut. A machine needs no lines. Handmades will be more irregular than those which are stamped out by machine.
2. There may be straight saw marks on the bottom. Circular came later.
3. Hand planing feels uneven to the touch. There may be sloping edges on the drawer bottom where it fits into side and front slots.
4. Friction causes drawers to wear down unevenly — more in the middle — after years of being yanked out half way. This shows on the bottom runners. The slides inside should show wear also.
5. Wear shows on other pieces. Chair rungs upon which sitters place their feet become smoothed off on top, and chair legs wear unevenly. When a broom hits a case piece, it leaves some mars. Places with body contact

159

show more wear, especially chair arms where hands rub continually. Sharp edges soften from dusting and use. Look for wear where it would occur naturally.

6. As wood ages the color deepens, and this is called patina. It should be distributed evenly over surfaces equally exposed to air, light, and dust. The bottom of the base drawer in desks or dressers gets more exposure than the top one and should be deeper in tone. If yellow shellac is used to provide pretend patina, this variation will not be present or the inside of the piece may be neglected completely, showing no "age darkening."

7. Old wood has an odor.

8. White glue is new and should not be present unless the piece has been recently repaired.

9. Squarish, not round, pegs should have a purpose, not be pounded in for looks. They held joints together and met needs nails do. Nails with square heads were used prior to 1870.

10. Study furniture styles and woods. Study hardware. That latter term includes hinges, locks, escutcheons (key hole plates), and handles whether they are wooden, porcelain, metal, or whatever. These give age clues, since various woods and styles of pulls occur more frequently in certain periods. Locks may have a patent date.

11. Thick wood (three fourth to an inch) and wide boards of various sizes, not one standard size, were utilized. Sometimes a top is one piece of wood or one large and one small board.

12. No one clue will provide the answer to a piece's age.

Incidentally, some people paint pieces to make them seem more elderly. New paint tends to peel, not flake. Here again, it's time to remove a drawer, the uppermost one. Examine the wood underneath the top of the case piece to determine the kind of wood used. It's tempting to buy a piece someone has painted because it usually sells at a bargain price, but this is a good way to camouflage a damaged top. If there are mars, stains, or burns present, the purchase is no bargain.

Many very fine copies of walnut tables, marble top bedroom sets, and cylinder secretary desks are on the market. Since marble stains readily, it should show some signs of age on an old piece and old glass in a secretary top may be wavy in appearance. Examine all before you buy. Tips help but knowledge, getting to know antiques, assists more.

Take courage. Everyone makes mistakes. Learn from your errors, but keep on buying and enjoying Victoriana.

# Glossary

**Applied**
an ornamentation crafted separately and applied to a piece later.

**Apron**
a connecting "skirt" on chairs, cabinets, and tables. It may be a structural aid or hide construction. The apron is found between the feet at the base of cabinets, cupboards, and chests. It is beneath a table top where the legs connect, or the portion under the seat of a chair. Not all tables and chairs have an apron. Also skirt.

**Arched Molding**
a half round convex strip used for trim.

**Armoire**
a large cupboard or wardrobe.

**Bail Handle**
a drawer pull with a loop pendant fastened to a back plate.

**Balloon Back**
a chair back which vaguely resembles an ascending hot air balloon in shape.

**Banding**
a strip of inlay which contrasts in color with the surrounding wood or a narrow border of veneering on drawer fronts.

**Beading**
a thin strip of molding which resembles small string of beads in a continuous line.

**Bevel**
a slanting edge cut on a board or sheet of glass.

**Breadboard Ends**
crosswise piece of wood fastened to the ends of furniture to prevent warping.

**Breakfront**
used on some bookcases, desks, wardrobes, and sideboards. The straight lines of the front are broken by a vertical portion which juts out.

**Broken Pediment**
a top ornament which does not meet completely at the apex (highest point).

**Burl**
an abnormal growth on trees which can be sliced thin to make decorative veneers.

**Cabriole Leg**
a leg with a double curve. It bulges at the knee, flows in and out again at the ankle.

**Cane**
long narrow strip of rattan used for weaving chair seats and backs.

**Canopy**
the framework on top of the tall posts of a bed which resembles a roof over the head. Also tester.

**Case Piece**
the box-like structure which encloses a cabinet, desk, chest of drawers, etc.

**Chamfer**
1.) an edge or corner cut off at a slant.
2.) a groove cut in wood.

**Cheval Glass**
a mirror which swings from vertical posts. (Cheval means horse in French, hence a support.)

**Chip Carving**
a simple carved ornamentation made with a chisel or gouge.

**Circa or C**
about, around a certain date. Circa 1900 means around 1900.

**Circular Molding**
an ornamental strip applied or carved on furniture in a circular or oval contour. May be incised or raised.

**Commode**

a washstand with an enclosed cupboard or drawers.

**Composition**

a mixture molded to resemble carving. It is often made from a plaster of Paris, rosin, sizing, and water mixture.

**Corner Stile**

the upright at the corner of a piece of furniture.

**Cornice**

the top horizontal molding on some pieces of furniture.

**Cottage Furniture**

factory made, inexpensive furniture produced in the mid- to late- 1800s and painted brightly with pastoral scenes. May be grained also.

**Crest or Cresting**

the ornamental top of a pediment, chair, or sofa back.

**Crotch-Grain Veneer**

a decorative "V" shaped strip of wood cut from the place where the branch intersects with the trunk of the tree and used as a covering over base woods.

**Cyma Curve**

a half convex, half concave continuous curve as seen in a cabriole leg.

**Davenport**

a small writing desk used during the 1800s. The sloping top lifts up so that articles can be stored within, and usually, the drawers pull out sideways instead of in the front.

**Demi-arm**

and hip rest are current terms which describe the partial arms on side chairs.

**Dowel**

a pin or peg which holds two pieces of wood together. Old pegs appear to be square, not round.

**Drop Front**

a hinged lid on a desk which drops down to form a writing surface.

**Dry Sink**

a cupboard with a well or tray in the top which was usually zinc lined. Used in the kitchen before water was piped into houses.

**Eastlake**

Charles Lock(e) Eastlake disliked the over-ornamented, cheaply made furniture the machine age was producing and wrote a book on household taste. He advocated conscious design in furniture and felt straight lines were more attractive, stronger, and used less wood than round shapes. Manufacturers took his rectangular lines and overdecorated them to produce an Eastlake style, circa 1870-1890.

**Ebony and Gilt Drops**

term from nineteenth century catalogues which describes drawer pulls now called "tear drop." An almost pear-shaped black pendant is attached to a round brass back plate.

**Eclectic**

copying, using, and adapting the designs and styles of previous periods.

**Escutcheon**

a fitting around a keyhole. Often made of brass or wood; it may be inset or applied.

**Etagère**

overly large and fancy whatnot with a mirror and shelves for displaying bric-a-brac.

**Extension Table**

the table top splits open so that additional leaves may be inserted to enlarge its surface.

**Fancy Chair**

almost any painted and decorated chair but especially Hitchcock and similar chairs.

**Fall Front**

a hinged flap on a desk which drops open to form a writing surface.

**Finger Grip**

a groove cut in the lower edge of a drawer front to use in place of a handle or knob.

**Finger Roll**

continuous concave molding cut into the frame of a chair or sofa.

**Finial**

a turned, carved, or cast end ornament on a clock, table, bedstead, post, or pediment.

**Flag**

marsh plant used to make chair seats. Also rush.

**Flush**

level with the surrounding surface.

**Fret or Fret work**

an ornamental border, perforated or cut in low relief.

**Gallery**

a raised railing of wood or metal around the top of a desk, table, sideboard, etc.

**Gateleg**
a swinging leg with a stretcher which serves as a support for a table leaf.

**Geometric**
a pattern made by interlacing circles, squares, triangles, and similar designs.

**Graining**
paint applied to resemble the grain of a specific wood.

**Hip Rest**
modern term for a partial arm on chairs; sometimes called demi-arm.

**Hitchcock**
the generic name for fancy chairs similar to those made by Lambert Hitchcock, circa 1820-50s.

**Incise**
design cut into or engraved into the surface.

**Inlay**
forming designs by inserting contrasting colors, grains, and textures flush in wood using wood, metal, shells, or ivory.

**Inset Pilaster**
an artificial, decorative pillar inserted in a flat surface, most frequently at the front corners of a case piece.

**Laminated**
layers of wood glued together with the grain of each succeeding layer at right angles to the ones adjacent. Makes a strong surface.

**Louis XV**
French style that emulated Louis XV (reigned 1715-1774). Elliptical shapes and graceful dainty curves. Cabriole leg. Floral carvings.

**Molding**
a continuous decorative edging applied to or carved into furniture.

**Ogee**
a molding with a double continuous curve.

**Panel**
a square or rectangular board held in place by a grooved framework. Sunken panel — beneath the framework. Flush — same height as the frame and usually molded. Raised — slightly above the surrounding surface, and frequently molded.

**Pediment**
an ornamental top on a piece of furniture.

**Pegged**
a wooden pin or dowel (peg) holds two pieces of board together at a joint. Old pegs appear square rather than round.

**Pendent Finial**
a downward finial.

**Pie Safe**
a closed cupboard with pierced tin, screening, or punched board panels which allowed air to circulate but helped keep rodents or flies off baked goods stored inside.

**Pier Glass or Mirror**
a tall narrow mirror often hung between two long windows.

**Pierced Carving**
open work carving.

**Pilaster**
a decorative artificial pillar with no structural strength set against a background. Often it is half round or rectangular.

**Projection Front**
a top that sticks out over the rest of the piece. A projecting top drawer overhangs the other drawers.

**Pull Brackets or Slides**
a pull out support used on a desk or secretary which has a drop-down writing surface.

**Raised Panel**
a panel which projects slightly above the surrounding surface and is often molded.

**Renaissance**
revival of interest in ancient Greek and Roman culture. Expressed in heavy ornamental furniture with elaborate carving and tall frames of the 1850-1885 time period.

**Ring Molding**
a circular ornamental edging applied to or carved into furniture.

**Rococo**
derived from French word for rock. Elaborate decorations based on natural objects such as rocks, shells, fruits, leaves, and flowers.

**Rounded End**
the curved, rather than straight, end of case pieces. A rounded "corner."

**Roundel**
any circular decorative disk such as a medallion or rosette.

**Rung**
the simple or decorative cross piece which connects chair, cabinet, or table legs at the bottom. A runner. Also stretcher.

## Runner

1.) another name for the rocker on a rocking chair.

2.) a guide strip to support a drawer.

3.) slides on which the drop fronts on desks are supported.

## Rush

a marsh plant used to make chair seats. Spirally rolled paper is a modern substitute. Also flag.

## Scalloped

a series of curves forming an ornamental edge derived from a shell (scallop) shape.

## Scribe Line

guide line incised by a cabinetmaker to show where and how two furniture pieces should be joined.

## Serpentine

snake-like. A wavy curve that is convex at the center and ends and concave between.

## Shaker

a celibate religious sect which crafted furniture with simple lines, attractive yet sturdy.

## Skirt

Frequently used as a decorative means to hide the construction of a piece, such as where the legs attach to a table top. Appears beneath the seat on chairs or near the base on cupboards, chests, and cabinets. Also apron.

## Slant Front

the hinged fall lid on a desk or secretary which provides a writing surface when dropped open and slants back when closed.

## Slat

1.) horizontal crossbars in chair backs.

2.) flat wooden supports placed between the rails of a bed to hold the spring and mattress.

3.) sometimes a rocker on a rocking chair is called a curved slat.

## Slip Seat

an upholstered seat which is removable.

## Spindle

slender rod in a chair back. Also stick.

## Splat

the center upright in a chair back which can be plain or decorative.

## Splay

slant out, especially chair legs which slant out from the seat to the floor.

164

## Spool Turning

resembles spools, knobs, balls, or like object strung together in a row.

## Stile

the vertical piece in a frame or panel in furniture.

## Stretchers

the rungs or crosspieces which connect cabinet table, or chair legs.

## Tape

strips of colored fabric used by Shakers to weave chair seats.

## Teapoy

small table for tea service.

## Tester

the roof-like framework on top of the tall posts of a bed. A half-tester covers the head only Also canopy.

## Tilt-top

a table top hinged to its base so it can be tipped to a vertical position.

## Tripod Table

table with a pedestal supported by three curved legs.

## Turning

shaping wood on a lathe with chisels; such a shaped piece.

## Urn

a decorative vase with a base used as a finial on furniture.

## Veneer

a thin layer of ornamental wood glued over the surface of a less expensive wood.

## Victorian Era

the years when Queen Victoria ruled England (1837-1901).

## Whatnot

a tier of shelves connected by turned posts used to display doodads. See etagère.

## Windsor Chairs

American Windsors have many slender back spindles. The legs are fitted into the seat without being framed by aprons (skirts).

# Bibliography

1. Aronson, Joseph, *Encyclopedia of Furniture,* New York, N.Y., Crown Publishers, Inc., 1965.

2. Bradford, Ernle, *Dictionary of Antiques,* London, England, The English Universities Press Ltd., 1963.

3. Century Furniture Company, *Furniture as Interpreted by the Century Furniture Company,* Grand Rapids, Michigan, 1926.

4. Grand Rapids Furniture Festival Souvenir Program, *Romance of Furniture,* Grand Rapids, Michigan, July 8, 9, 10, 1936.

5. Grotz, George, *The New Antiques,* Garden City, N.Y., Doubleday & Company, 1964.

6. Miller, Robert W., *Clock Guide No. 2,* Des Moines, Iowa, Wallace-Homestead Book Company, 1976.

7. Nelson, Matter & Co., Catalogue, *Manufacturers of Furniture,* Grand Rapids, Michigan, January 1st, 1873.

8. Nelson, Matter & Co., Catalogue, *Manufacturers of Furniture,* Grand Rapids, Michigan, March, 1876.

9. Nesbit, Wilbur D., *The Story of Berkey & Gay,* Reprinted, with slight additions, from *Musey's Magazine* of September, 1911.

10. Norbury, James, *The World of Victoriana,* London, England, Hamlyn, 1972.

11. *Oak Furniture Styles and Prices,* Des Moines, Iowa, Wallace-Homestead Book Company, 1975. .

12. Ormsbee, Thomas H., *Field Guide to American Victorian Furniture,* Boston, Mass., Little, Brown and Company, 1952.

13. Ransom, Frank Edward, *The City Built on Wood, a History of the Furniture Industry in Grand Rapids, Michigan,* Ann Arbor, Michigan, Edwards Bros., Inc., 1955.

14. Shull, Thelma, *Victorian Antiques,* Rutland, Vermont, Charles E. Tuttle Company, 1963.

15. Symonds, R. W., and Whineray, B. B., *Victorian Furniture,* London, Country Life Limited, 1962.

16. Winchester, Alice, *How To Know American Antiques,* The New American Library, New York, N.Y., 1951.

# Index